Law Firm Digital Marketing Made Easy

The Only Book You'll Ever Need to Become A Best-Known Attorney

Josh Konigsberg

ISBN-13: 978-0-578-89263-4

Printed in the U.S.A.

Editing: Daria Anne DiGiovanni

Cover Design: Zeljka Kojic

Dedication

To my loving mother, who taught me that
love and compassion is the path.

And to my two children, who are my motivation.
Daddy loves you every day!

Table of Contents

INTRODUCTION

A Category of One – Your Online Marketing Plan for Dominating the WEB –Website, SEO, PPC, Pay-Per-Lead Services, LSAs, and More!

Congratulations on your purchase of *Law Firm Digital Marketing Made Easy: The Only Book You'll Ever Need to Become A Best-Known Attorney*, a complete overview of what it takes to maximize potential client contact, generate leads, and create a unique digital omnipresence for your law firm that puts you in a category of one.

There are several channels and mediums to consider for your business when you investigate online and digital marketing. For this book's purpose, we will use the terms "online," "digital," and "internet" interchangeably.

I wrote this book with your law firm's marketing needs in mind, regardless of your area of law; however, I make distinctions in each section about the various PPC, SEO, and LSA options that might impact your specific area of law.

At first glance, the marketing options available in your online marketing plan could seem overwhelming, even if you are familiar with many of the current platforms in use. We can help you navigate the ever-growing number of digital marketing tools and social media outlets you need to position your firm for success in a competitive market.

Digital marketing optimization opportunities include:

- Search Engines (Google, Bing, Yahoo, DuckDuckGo, and on those search engines; Maps, Organic, Pay-Per-Click)
- Social Media (Facebook, Instagram, Twitter, LinkedIn)
- Online Business Listing Directories - Generic (YP, Yelp.com, etc.)
- Online Vertical Directories - (Lawyers.com, FindLaw, Avvo. etc.)

To maximize your lead flow from the internet, you must develop an effective plan that optimizes the use of each of these online marketing opportunities.

Throughout this book, we lay the foundation to:

- ❖ Map out your online marketing plan (Website, SEO, PPC, Pay-Per-Lead services, etc.).
- ❖ Start with the fundamentals (Market, Message, Media) before jumping headfirst into your Internet Marketing Strategy.
- ❖ Set up your website for success.
- ❖ Understand how search engines work, and discover the differences between the paid, organic, and map listings.
- ❖ For **Search Engine Optimization** (SEO) - How to optimize your website with keywords that are most important in guiding clients to your law firm.
- ❖ Help you build on our developed framework:
    - ➢ How to conduct keyword research.

- Our list of the most commonly searched keywords broken down by industry.
- How to achieve the maximum result by mapping out the pages that should be included on your website.
- How to optimize your website for ranking in the organic listings on major search engines.
- How to improve your website's visibility so you can rank on page one for your most important keywords.
- List of link-building techniques and strategies proven to enhance rankings even after Search Engine algorithm updates.
- Content marketing strategies for maintaining relevance in your market.

❖ Optimize Google Maps - How to get ranked on the Google Map in your area.

- The fundamentals of Google Maps ranking (NAP, Citations, Links, and Reviews).
- How to establish a strong name, address, and phone number profile.
- How to claim and optimize your Google Business Profile Local Listing.
- How to develop authority for your map listing via citation development.
- List of the top citation sources for your Law Firm, according to your industry standards.

- How to get genuine reviews from your customers in your service area:
    - Sample Review Capture Page
    - Sample Review Request Email
    - Sample Review Follow up process

- Understand Website Conversion Fundamentals - How to ensure that your website converts visitors into leads in the form of calls and web form submissions.

- Learn the importance of reviews and ratings for the overall health of your website and digital footprint.

- Understand Mobile Optimization - How to optimize your website for mobile visitors.

- Utilize Social Media Marketing - How to utilize Social Media (Facebook, Instagram, Twitter, LinkedIn, and other social platforms for maximum effect in your business.

- Use Video Marketing - How to tap into the power of YouTube and other video sharing websites to enhance your visibility and drive better conversion.

- Leverage email marketing tools (Constant Contact, Mail Chimp, etc.) to connect with your customers on a deeper level, receive more reviews, get more social media connections and ultimately get repeat and referral business.

- Understand and capitalize on Paid Online Advertising opportunities.

- Use Pay-Per-Click Marketing (Google Ads and Bing Ads) - How to maximize the profitability of your Pay-Per-Click Marketing efforts.
    - Why PPC should be part of your overall online marketing strategy
    - Why most PPC campaigns fail
    - Understanding the Google Ads Auction process
    - How to configure and manage your Pay-Per-Click campaign for maximum ROI
- Use Paid Online Directories - What paid online directories should you consider advertising in (Martindale-Hubbell, Lawyers.com, Yahoo, Yelp, Yellow Pages, etc.).
- Track, Measure and Quantify - How to track your online marketing plan to ensure your investment generates a strong return.

Chapter One will briefly touch on the various internet marketing channels and then I'll go into more detail throughout the book. Let it guide you by creating your digital marketing plan and serving as your roadmap moving forward.

CHAPTER ONE

Online Marketing Channels – Creating a Digital Footprint for Your Law Firm. What's in Your Toolbox?

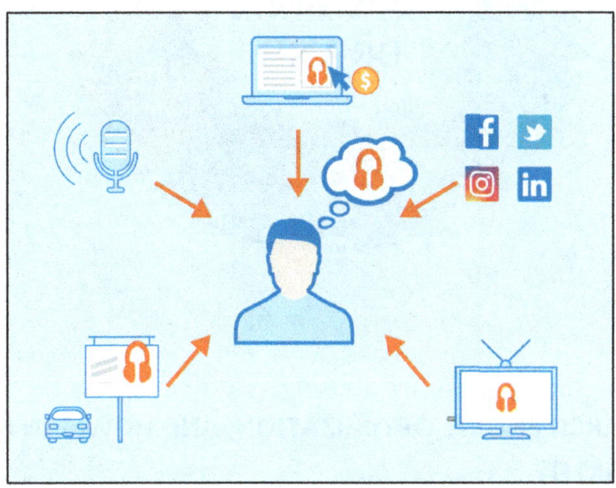

1. Search Engine Optimization (Organic Listings and Map Listings)
2. PPC on Google Ads and Bing Ads Network
3. Reviews and Reputation Marketing
4. Social Media Marketing (Facebook, Instagram, Twitter, LinkedIn)
5. Video Marketing
6. Email Marketing

7. Paid Directory Marketing (Martindale-Hubbell, Lawyers.com, Yahoo, Yelp, Yellow Pages, etc.)

WHAT IS SEARCH ENGINE OPTIMIZATION, AND HOW CAN MY FIRM BENEFIT FROM IT?

Search Engine Optimization (SEO) is the process of increasing your company's visibility on the Search Engine Results Page (SERP) on major search engines (Google, Yahoo, Bing, etc.) in the organic, non-paid listings as consumers search for lawyers that practice in your area of law.

There are three critical components of the SERP:

1. Paid Listings – The area along the top and side that advertisers can bid on and pay for to obtain decent placement in the search engines

2. Organic Listings – The area in the body of the Search Engine Results Page
3. Map Listings – These are the listings that come up beneath the paid listings and above the organic listings in many searches

For our purposes, we discuss Paid Listings in the next section.

Search Engine Optimization involves getting your website to show up in the SERP for Organic and Map Listings. These listings account for a majority of the search volume. According to research from Zero Limit Web, the first five organic results account for 67.60 percent of clicks in Google.

Most people associate internet marketing exclusively with Search Engine Optimization. However, you will begin to see that SEO is only a tiny piece of the MUCH BIGGER internet marketing puzzle for business owners and law firms.

SEARCH ENGINE MARKETING

Pay-Per-Click

Now that we have discussed SEO let's talk about Search Engine Marketing or PPC (Pay-Per-Click). Google, Yahoo, and Bing offer paid programs that allow you to BUY listings associated with your keywords to be placed in designated areas of their sites.

There are four essential benefits of PPC:

1. It's much faster than SEO. Your keyword listings will appear on search engines almost immediately.
2. You only pay when someone clicks on your listing – hence the term pay-per-click marketing.

3. You can turn it off and on as needed. You can increase your exposure by increasing your click spend and thus get more clicks, or you can pause it if you get too busy.
4. Your ad can show up in a larger regional and national geographic area, in the regions and cities in which you want your ideal clients to see you and find you.

PPC Marketing is exceptionally complicated, but to oversimplify it, it works on an auction or bidding system similar to eBay. You simply choose your keywords and propose a bid for the amount of money you would be willing to pay for each click. We can help you determine which options are best suited to your needs.

Several factors determine placement, which I will discuss in detail in the PPC chapter. But, in the broadest sense, the one who is willing to pay the most per click will be rewarded the top position in the search engines, while the second-most will be in the second position, and so on.

PPC Marketing is an excellent strategy to get your law firm's website to appear at the top of the search engines right away and drive qualified traffic to your website.

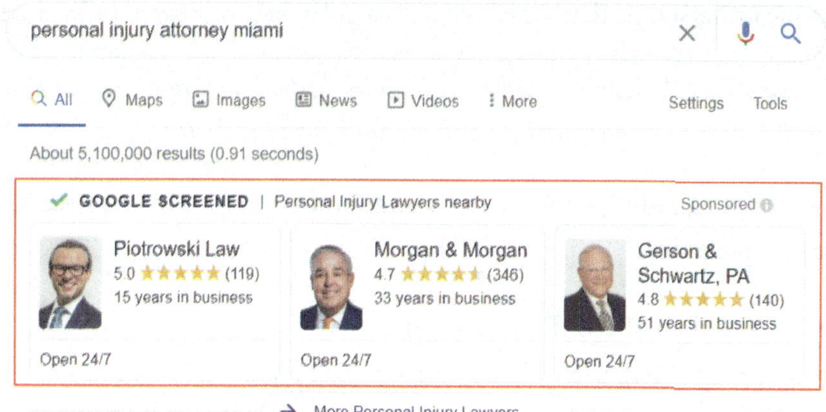

SOCIAL MEDIA MARKETING

Getting to know your clientele and developing connections

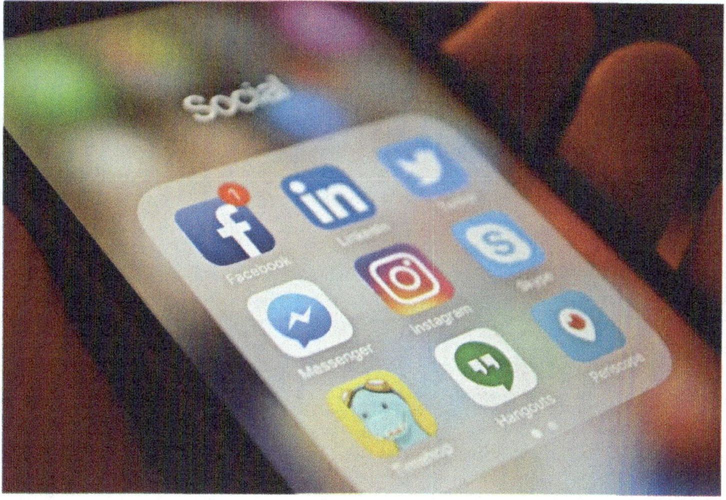

Social Media platforms like Facebook, Instagram, Twitter, LinkedIn, and YouTube have generated significant buzz. Since our area of expertise is the digital marketplace, we have developed strategies to show you how these forums can be used for both new firms and firms that have been established over time.

Everyone understands that social media is a great way to grow your business.

This book covers the essential information and methods for effectively tapping into social media forums to drive traffic to your firm's website.

The statistics regarding online activity and internet traffic around Facebook alone are staggering:

- More than 500 million active users
- 50% of active users log on to Facebook on any given day
- The average user has 130 connections
- People spend over 700 billion minutes per month on Facebook

How can you employ this fantastic tool to grow your business and use it to connect with your sphere of influence, connect with established clients, and attract new ones?

Using social media, you can solidify and maintain existing relationships, remain top-of-mind, ***FRONT AND CENTER*** in the digital sphere, and increase repeat and referral business.

VIDEO MARKETING

Dynamic visuals create a personal connection that generates trust and triggers memory.

Place yourself front and center by creating a video.

Did you know YouTube is the second-most used search engine on the market? Would you guess it is even ahead of Bing and Yahoo? It's true.

Millions of people conduct YouTube searches daily; however, most business owners tend to focus solely on SEO and neglect the opportunities afforded them by video and YouTube.

By implementing a Video Marketing Strategy for your law firm, you can achieve additional placement in search results for your keywords, enhance the effectiveness of your SEO efforts, and improve visitor conversion.

Videos that introduce your firm to consumers enhance repeat business and word-of-mouth networking. Vibrant visuals maximize the chances of them remembering you and your firm's name.

EMAIL MARKETING FOR LAW FIRMS

Develop communication channels to enhance client access

Like social media marketing, email marketing provides an effective method of remaining top-of-mind with your clients and increasing repeat business and referrals. Compared to direct mail and newsletters, email marketing remains the most cost-effective means to communicate with your clients.

As we will discuss in the **Email Marketing for Law Firms** chapter, you can use email marketing to draw your clients into your social media sphere.

PAID DIRECTORY MARKETING

Establish your firm as the persistent, reliable place for clients to go for legal assistance

For law firms, multiple online directories are vital to success, including:

1. Martindale-Hubbell
2. Lawyers.com
3. FindLaw.com
4. Avvo.com
5. SuperLawyers.com

Now that you understand each of the internet marketing channels available, we will discuss how you can leverage them to connect with new clients and grow your business in the following chapters.

WHERE TO START?

Creating and Maintaining an Omnipresence in the digital marketplace

With a nearly infinite amount of internet marketing channels, where should you start?

Achieving positive outcomes, acquiring clients, and maintaining a foothold in the digital marketing realm requires instituting each of these online marketing opportunities over time.

However, you must first begin with the foundation: your website, organic rankings, and social media/email. Begin by investigating the various paid marketing opportunities once you set your website up correctly, rank on search engines for your most important keywords in the organic, non-paid listings, and have established active and consistent engagement on social media.

We have found that the most impactful opportunity to get ranked organically lies in the non-paid listings through intensive research and use. From there, you can leverage the additional profits in paid marketing to further augment your growth.

Once you rank well organically, you can start to run a well-managed pay-per-click campaign and explore paid online directory listings on Lawyers.com, Martindale-Hubbell, etc. We can help you determine which venues are best suited to your firm's area of law.

Next, let's look at the fundamentals of your overall marketing strategy before pressing forward into implementing the methods Law Firm Marketing Pros has developed to ensure your success.

CHAPTER TWO

Start with the Fundamentals – Market, Message, Media – Before Jumping Headfirst Into Your Internet Marketing Strategy

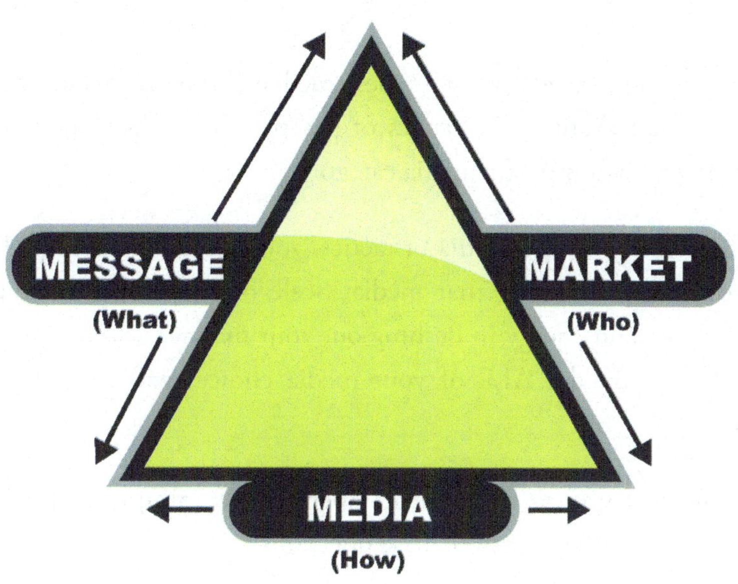

Before we delve into internet marketing, SEO, and social media marketing, let's first confirm we have built a strong marketing foundation.

As I talk with various law firms across the United States, I have realized that the majority skip past the fundamentals of their marketing strategy and dive headfirst into tactics (pay-per-click advertising, SEO, social media, etc.).

What do I mean when I say "fundamentals"?

All marketing has three core components:

1. Message (what)
2. Market (who)
3. Media (how)

You must have a unique message: who you are, what you do, what makes you unique, and why someone should hire you rather than another law firm that offers the same service.

You must define your market: your ideal clients to whom you promote your services.

Finally, you must investigate your best media: the places where you can reach your ideal clients. The tactics of pay-per-click, SEO, social media, direct mail, etc., fall into the media category.

If you focus solely on the media or tactics, you will likely fail regardless of your precision in selecting that media. Scale back to the fundamentals. Invest the time and energy in fleshing out your message and defining your market. Once you do, ALL of your media choices will be much more effective.

What is the best way to go about it? Spend a few minutes and THINK. Take out a notepad and answer these questions:

MESSAGE

- What do I do that is unique and different from my competitors? For example, do you offer a guaranteed time frame for your appointments? Do you offer flat fees as an intellectual property attorney? Free consultations to discuss their case?

- Consider the psychology of a consumer and their concerns about hiring a new law firm. They may be thinking, "They're so busy, they'll probably treat me like a number or hand my case off to a less experienced attorney," or "They are going to nickel-and-dime me for every email and phone call."

- How can you address your clients' common concerns uniquely?

MARKET

- Who is my ideal client? Please realize not everyone resides in your city nor within a 25-mile radius of your office. You must be clear about the audience you want to attract.

- Analyze your last 25 customers to evaluate who spent the most money, had the highest profit margins, and expressed genuine satisfaction with your service. What are the unique characteristics of these good clients? Do they live in a particular area of town? Do they have a higher income level? How did they hear about your legal services?

- Start to define your ideal client to put a marketing plan in place to attract similar clients.

Once you have fleshed out your message and market, you can turn your attention to the best media. To determine the most effective media for you, consider where you can reach your ideal client.

The internet is an excellent place to connect with ideal clients who are in the market for your services. Throughout the remainder of this book, we will explain the various internet marketing channels and how you can use them to engage with your qualified prospects.

Remember, start with the FUNDAMENTALS (Message, Market, and Media) before running headstrong into any marketing.

CHAPTER THREE

How to Set Up Your Website for Success

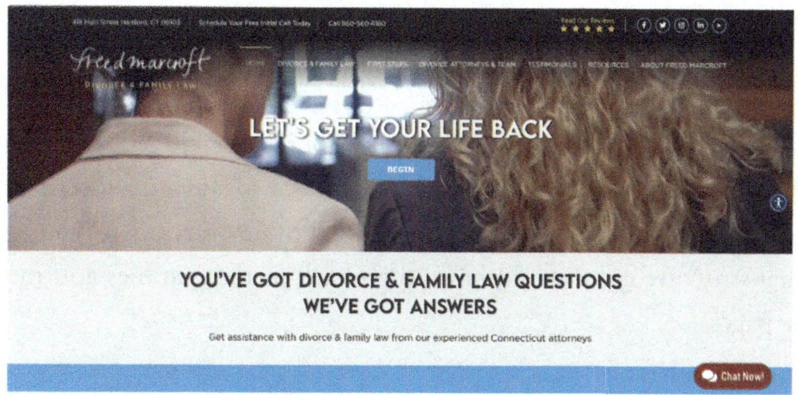

This chapter focuses on how to set up your website. In later chapters, we will cover many details about SEO, Google Maps optimization, pay-per-click marketing, etc. However, if you do not have a properly designed and functioning website, you will waste your efforts. Before you can or even should begin exploring your digital marketing options, you must have a website.

FORMATS

Below are the website formats and options available:

1. **HTML Site** – You can incorporate basic HTML pages and individual pages into your website, which is how most people built websites several years ago. They hyper-linked multiple pages together.

2. **Template-Based Site Builders** – You can obtain site builders through providers such as GoDaddy, Website by Tonight, and IONOS by 1&1 by buying your domain and setting up your website. Because you don't have much control or flexibility, this type is less than ideal. Regardless, there are many sites in this format.

3. **CMS (Content Management Systems)** – Some examples include WordPress, Joomla, and Drupal, the major players in this category.

A content management system (CMS) is ideal for a business because it offers scalability. In any of these platforms, you can change your navigation as desired, add as many pages as you need, and scale-out your site quickly.

If you build your website via Website by Tonight or HTML format with graphics behind the website, every time you want to add a new section, you would have to start from scratch. To add the new section to your navigational structure, you would have to go back to the graphics and modify all the pages.

With a CMS, everything is built behind code, giving you the ability to apply easy edits and add multiple pages. As you will see in the book's search engine optimization section, your website can dedicate a page for each one of your legal services and each city in which you operate.

A CMS allows you to create your pages in a scalable format without messing around with the graphics or doing anything difficult to control. It is easy to access, modify, and update. Using formats like WordPress and Joomla, you may access the back-end administrative dashboard at *yourcompany.com/login.*

After entering your username and password, you will find an easy-to-edit system with pages and posts that function similarly to Microsoft Word. You can input text, import images, and press "save," thus updating all new edits on your live website.

Content Management Systems feature intelligently structured linking between pages and content, making them significantly search engine friendly. Based on our years of experience, this method is superior to regular HTML or Website by Tonight.

In many cases, a blog will be automatically bolted onto a CMS-based website, providing you with a section in which you can post updates. In the SEO chapter, we cover the importance of blogging regularly.

Another benefit of content management systems is that they provide various plugins you can choose to incorporate on your website. For example, you can easily pull in your social media feeds, YouTube Videos, and check-ins.

You may also syndicate your website to post any new updates to your social media profiles and add map integration where people can click to either get instructions or view a map to determine the areas that your organization serves. CMS offers a surplus of features that a non-CMS type option does not.

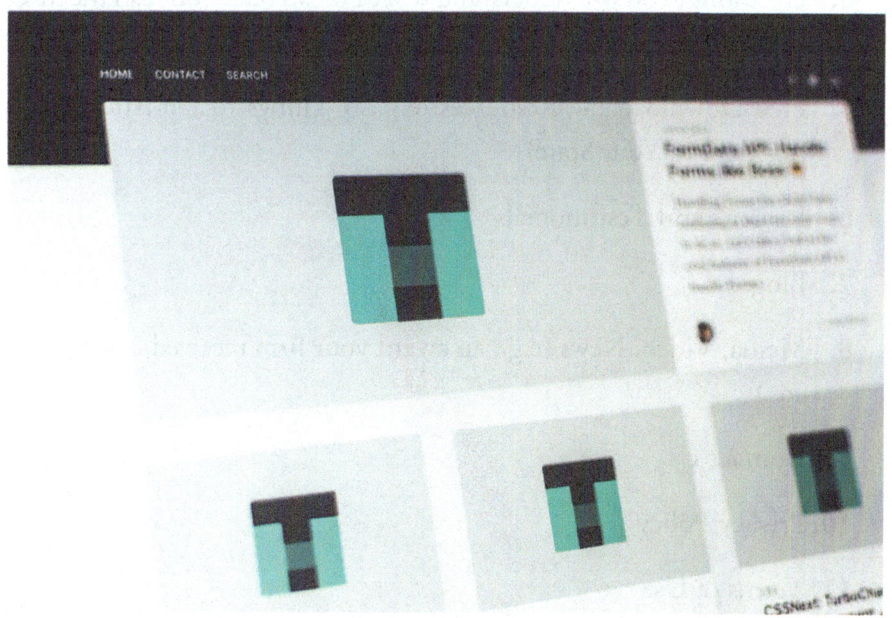

Whether you want to build a website from the ground up or need a redesign, I recommend CMS, ideally in WordPress, the most adopted website platform available. User-friendly and fantastic, developers constantly update and improve WordPress, which I have found to work well for multiple businesses and law firms. For these reasons, you have my stamp of approval to build your website on a WordPress platform.

WHAT SHOULD YOUR WEBSITE INCLUDE?

What pages should your website have? What navigation structure should you create? Depending on your type of law firm, you will need to showcase different things. For most firms, though, the basics should be:

1. Home
2. About Us
3. Practice Areas
4. Locations (You will understand what I mean once you read the SEO Chapter)
5. Free Downloadable Resources (e.g., 5 Things to Do After A Car Accident in Your State)
6. Reviews and Testimonials
7. Blog
8. Media, Video, News (e.g., an award your firm received, a new hire, etc.)
9. Contact Us
10. Privacy Policy
11. Terms of Use

These are the core pages. Within "About Us," you might incorporate a drop-down menu for subcategories, including "Meet the Team," "Why Choose Our Firm," etc.

You want to drive people back to a "Why Choose Us" section. If you struggle to recruit and retain high-quality talent, consider adding a "Careers" page under the "About Us" navigation. That will provide visitors the option to complete an application and learn more about your organization.

Within "Our Services," add a drop-down that lists the types of legal services you offer. We discuss this to a great extent in the SEO chapter. Include landing pages for each of your services, optimized with different keyword combinations.

A "Reviews and Testimonials" page provides a section to showcase what your clients say about you in text or video form. You can also pull in reviews from sites such as Google Maps, Martindale-Hubbell, and Lawyers.com. Finally, you will need a "Contact Us" page where web visitors can obtain your general contact information. These are core elements for your website.

A Clear Description of Who You Are

A visitor who stumbles upon your website shouldn't have to do a thorough investigation to figure out who you are and what you do. That's why it's essential to mention your law firm name and sum up your practice areas above your website's fold section. A clear and specific description will attract the visitor's attention within two to three seconds and encourage them to spend time on your website.

Your Primary Contact Details

Outside of your navigational structure, what else should your website feature? What other elements help with conversion?

Always provide a primary phone number on every page of your website, in the upper right-hand corner. When somebody visits a page, their eyes are naturally drawn to the website's top section, where they can see the logo and the phone number. People expect the phone number to be somewhere in this location; therefore, it is ideal to place a prominent phone number, encouraging them to "call now" to schedule a consultation.

An Obvious Call to Action

Business websites should always make a web form available from which a potential client can quickly request a call or a meeting. Bear in mind that every visitor to your website is in a different situation and frame of mind. You may have someone who's on their phone or leisurely looking to contact you for your legal services and can pick up the phone to call you.

On the other hand, somebody in a work environment may not have the ability to stop what they are doing and make a phone call without drawing attention from their coworkers. However, they may be able to browse around online to find out what options are available.

Your potential customers may reach your website and feel torn between making a call right now, scheduling the appointment, or wanting to have someone from your team contact them. Make it easy for them to enter their information into a web form where they can provide their name, phone number, email address, and a note detailing their requests that they can send online. It makes it easier and doesn't create any pressure.

Social Media Links

Provide links to your social media profiles. Link to Facebook, Twitter, and LinkedIn so customers can quickly jump off, engage with you on social media, see what you're doing, and press that important "like," "follow," or "subscribe" button. It helps create a sense of authenticity when your clients can see your social media content.

Customer Testimonials

Provide a direct link that drives visitors to your online reviews and testimonials. Post your credentials either in the sidebar or in the header graphic, proving, for example, that you're a member of your local and state bar association. Such trust symbols allow potential customers to rest assured that you are a credible law firm. You're involved in the community and more apt to provide them with excellent service. They'll feel more comfortable doing business with you.

You must include your law firm name, address, and phone number on every page of your website. As I explain in the Google Maps Optimization chapter, a consistent name, address, and phone number are critical for ranking on Google Maps. Ideally, your name, address, and phone number should appear in the footer section. Your contact information must display on all of your pages, including the Contact Us page, of course.

Authentic Images

You must infuse personality into your website with authentic photos and videos. Showcase your law firm: feature yourself, the founder and attorney, and your staff, including the other attorneys, paralegals, administrative assistants, etc.

Showcase the office itself. Don't use stock photography, but authentic imagery to give the visitor the chance to get to know, like, and trust you before they even pick up the phone. I've seen this tactic prove itself time and time again.

Suppose a potential client visited two different law firm sites for a similar area of law. One of them is generic, the same image they have seen before with the exact attorney and client. On the other hand, the other website features a genuine picture of the actual attorney(s) and the rest of the team.

An authentic page like this converts 10 to 1. You must let your real personality resonate through the website.

You must also craft messaging that explains why they should choose your law firm. Why should someone retain you over the competition? Guide them down a path to learn more about why you are their best option, where they can see your online reviews, and if they're on the fence, where they can locate some unique resources, such as a free download, that will drive action. This kind of bait will compel them to contact you right away, as opposed to continuing to browse the web for another lawyer.

Mobile Website

The other major factor you want to address from a conversion perspective is a mobile-ready version of your website. More and more people access the internet via smartphones such as iPhones and Androids. Make sure the mobile version of your site isn't the same as your regular site.

Your mobile website should be condensed to fit their screen and give them the information they need. It should integrate with their phone, so all they have to do is press a button to call you.

People searching or accessing your website from a mobile device are in a different state of mind than those who browse and find you on a computer. Make it easy for them to obtain the information they need and get in touch with you.

CHAPTER FOUR

Understanding HOW Search Engines Work and the Differences Between the Paid, Organic, and Map Listings

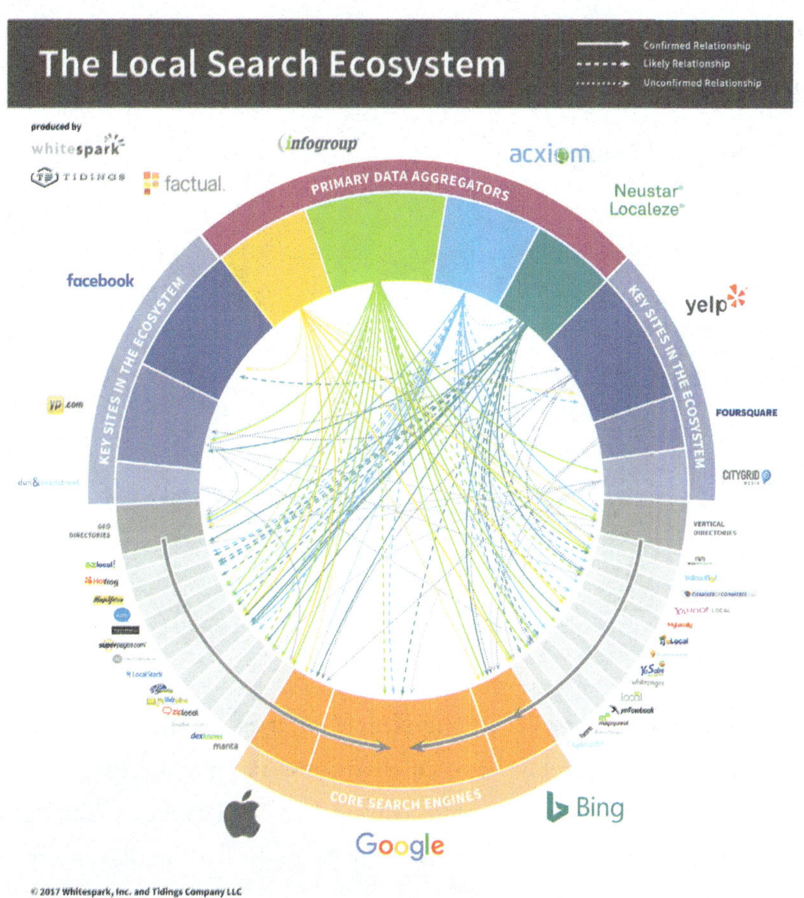

This section demystifies the search engines and breaks down the Search Engine Results Page's anatomy. Google's ultimate goal is to provide trusted information to the consumer. Why? Because if the consumer does not trust the information Google provides, they will go somewhere else. Everything Google and other search engines do revolve around providing trusted and relevant information.

By understanding how each component works to provide trusted and relevant information, you can formulate a strategy to maximize your ranking results.

There are three core components of the Search Engines Results page:

1. Paid/PPC Listings
2. Map Listings
3. Organic Listings

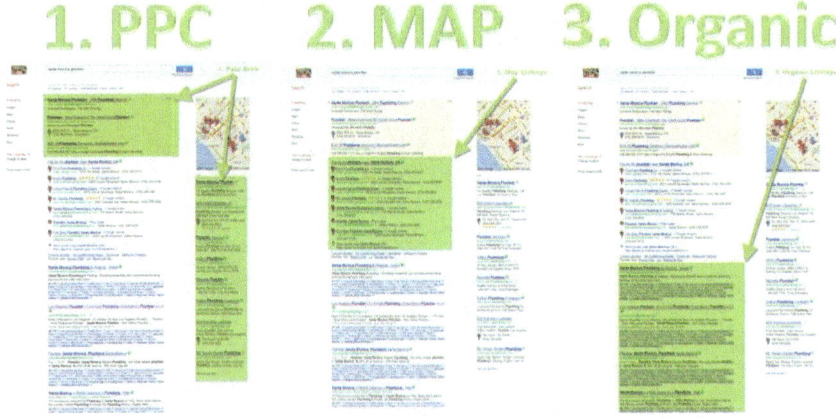

1. *Paid/PPC Listings* – In the search engines' paid section, you can select keywords relevant to your business and pay to be listed among the search results. It is referred to as PPC or Pay-Per-Click because rather than paying a flat monthly or daily fee for placement, you simply pay each time someone clicks on the link.

2. *Map Listings/Google Business Profile (GBP) Listings* – The map listings have become very important because they are the first thing that comes up in search results for most locally-based searches after the ads. If someone searches for some particular area of law in your geographic market, chances are the first thing they look at will be the map listings. Unlike the search engine's paid section, you can't buy your way into the Map Listings. You must earn it. Once you do, there is no per-click cost associated with being in this section of the search engine.
3. *Organic Listings* – The organic/natural section of the Search Engine Results page appears directly beneath the Map Listings in many local searches but appears directly beneath the Paid Listings in the absence of the Map Listings (the Map Section only shows up in specific local searches). Like the Map Listings, you can't pay your way into this section of the search engines, and there is no per-click cost associated with it. The challenge is that you're competing with business listing directories and vertical directories that typically occupy 40-60% of the organic listings.

Now that you understand the three major components of the Search Engine Results and the differences between Paid Listings, Map Listings, and Organic Listings, you might wonder: "What section is the most important?"

Many law firms ask us this question every day.

The fact is all three components are essential, and each should have a place in your online marketing program because you want to show up as often as possible when someone is searching for your service offerings in your area.

RETURN ON INVESTMENT

With that said, every law firm has budgetary constraints, so we're going to assume you are operating on a limited marketing budget. You want to make each digital marketing dollar count by focusing your investment on the sections that drive the strongest Return on Investment (ROI).

Research indicates that the vast majority of the population looks directly at the Organic and Map Listings when searching. Their eyes simply glance over the Paid Listings (as illustrated by the images below).

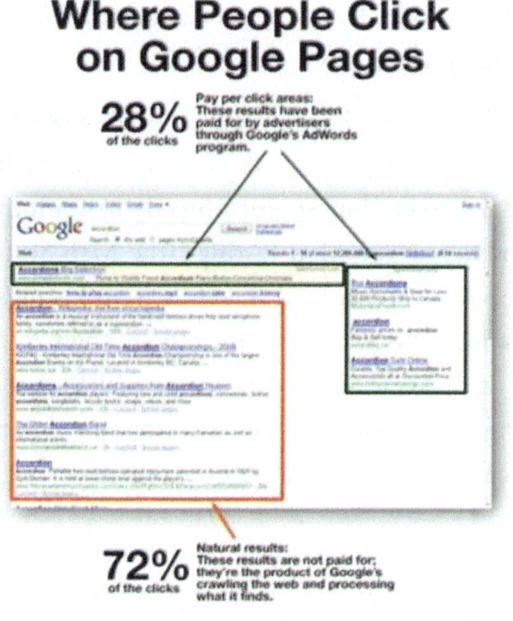

Data from Fredrick Marckini's Search Engine Strategies 2008 Toronto keynote.

If you are operating on a limited budget and need to get the best bang for your buck, start by focusing your efforts on the area which receives the most clicks at the lowest cost. We have found placement in the Organic and Map section on the Search Engines drives a SIGNIFICANTLY higher Return on Investment than Pay-Per-Click Marketing. However, organic and maps take longer to rank on Page One.

Begin with the Organic Listings, and then, as you increase your profits, you can start to shift those dollars into a proactive Pay-Per-Click Marketing effort.

In the next chapter, we will start to look at Search Engine Optimization and how to optimize your website to rank in the organic listings (non-paid) for the most critical keywords in your field.

HOW DO SEARCH ENGINES WORK?

It is also essential to understand how search engines work, including the process of crawling and indexing and the concept of page rank.

Search engines work by crawling billions of web pages using their web crawlers or web spiders. These web crawlers are also known as Search engine bots.

Understanding Search Engine Index

As Google explains:

"The crawling process begins with a list of web addresses from past crawls and sitemaps provided by website owners. As our crawlers visit these websites, they use links on those sites to discover other pages. The software pays special attention to new sites, changes to existing sites, and dead links. Computer programs determine which sites to crawl, how often, and how many pages to fetch from each site.

"We offer Search Console to give site owners granular choices about how Google crawls their site: they can provide detailed instructions about how to process pages on their sites, can request a recrawl, or can opt-out of crawling altogether using a file called "robots.txt." Google never accepts payment to crawl a site more frequently — we provide the same tools to all websites to ensure the best possible results for our users."

Once a search engine discovers a webpage, it adds it to a search engine data structure called index. Search engine index includes all the crawled web URLs (your website address), along with several critical vital elements about the content of each web URL such as:

- ✔ The keywords
- ✔ Type of content
- ✔ The uniqueness of the page
- ✔ User engagement with the page

Understanding Search Engine Algorithm

The search engine algorithm aims to display a relevant set of high-quality search results to fulfill the user's search query as quickly as possible.

What Happens When a User Enters a Search Query?

When a user/consumer/browser enters a search query into the search engine, the search engine tries to identify all the pages which are deemed relevant. During this process, the search engine uses a unique algorithm to hierarchically rank the most relevant pages into a set of results. The algorithm used to rank the most relevant web pages differs for each search engine.

For example, a web page that ranks on the top for a search query in Google may not rank highly for the same question in Bing. Mentioned below are a few elements search engines use to return the results.

- ✔ Search query
- ✔ Location
- ✔ Language detected
- ✔ Previous search history
- ✔ The device from which the user entered the search query

CHAPTER FIVE

Search Engine Optimization – How to Optimize Your Website for the Keywords That Are Most Important for Your Law Firm

Getting your company listed in the organic section (non-paid listings) of the search engines comes down to two core factors:

- Establishing the **proper on-page optimization** so Google knows who you are, what areas of law you practice, and the general geographic area you serve. Effective content and keyword use allows Google to put in the index for the right keywords. You do this by creating pages for each of your practice areas and then optimizing them for specific keyword combinations (Ex. Your City + family law, Your City + child custody, Your City + child support, etc.).

- Creating enough **authority and transparency** so Google ranks you on page one (rather than page ten) for those specific keywords. Ultimately, it comes down to having credible inbound links and citations from other websites to your website and its sub-pages. He who has the most credible inbound links, citations, and reviews will be the most successful.

Throughout this chapter, I provide specific how-to information on precisely what pages to add to your business website - and why. I also discuss what you can do to improve your authority/transparency in Google's eyes so your website ranks on page one for the keywords which are most important to your business.

Before you start creating pages and trying to do the "on-page optimization" work, you must clarify the most commonly searched keywords relative to the legal services you offer.

By understanding the keywords, you can optimize your website for the words that will actually drive qualified traffic to your site. One needs to conduct detailed research of the market and the requirements that potential clients must identify the optimal keywords which will help you bring in more qualified clients.

Given that different law firms might be working in different areas of law, it is imperative they learn the methodology behind selecting the most relevant keywords for their services. We have provided an overview of how to conduct keyword research.

How to Conduct Keyword Research

To determine what your potential clients are searching for when they need your services, here are a number of tools that can be used to conduct keyword research.

Note: Some are free of charge while others have a monthly cost associated with them. Some of the **better keyword research tools include Google AdWords Keyword Tool, WordStream, and SEM Rush.**

For this book's purpose, we have developed instructions based on the free Google AdWords Keyword Tool. To use the Google AdWords Keyword Tool, you'll need to:

- Develop a list of your services and case types and save it in a Word document
- Develop a list of the cities that you operate in (your primary city of service and the smaller surrounding towns) or that you want cases from, and save it in a Word document (it can be part of the same document)
- Go to https://app.kwfinder.com/

- Enter your keyword
- Enter a city
- Click "Find Keywords"
- You will have to get your results for each city via a separate search process. You cannot get results for more than one city at a time. You may have to do this multiple times.

- You will now see a list of each of your keywords with a "search volume" number beside it
- Download the list as a CSV and convert it to an Excel file
- Sort the list from most significant to smallest

You now have a list of the most commonly searched keywords in the area for the case types you want, in the cities from which you want them. With this list, you can map out keywords to specific pages on your website, and rest assured that you base your strategy on opportunity rather than a rough estimate.

MOST COMMONLY SEARCHED INDUSTRY KEYWORDS

Below is a list of the most searched keywords broken down by some of the most common areas of law. **Your firm will want to focus on those keywords most relevant to your area of law, keeping in mind that you may have generalized keywords that are also useful.**

Most Searched Law Keywords in the United States:

Keyword	Volume
Lawyer	216,000
Attorney	155,000
Lawyers near me	110,000
Immigration lawyer	74,000
Personal injury lawyer	69,500

Car accident lawyer	69,500
Divorce lawyer	46,500
Law firms	38,000
Family lawyer	43,500
Real estate law attorney	300
Personal injury attorney	49,500
Business lawyer	19,400
Tax attorney	12,100
Auto accident lawyer	19,400

Based on this data, in order to get the most from the internet from an SEO perspective, you will want to create content on your website for the following keyword combinations:

Note: adding "near me" should be a common practice due to the significant increase in near me searches over this past year.

Your City + Lawyer
Your City + attorney
Your City + Immigration lawyer
Your City + Lawyers
Your City + Personal injury lawyer
Your City + Car accident lawyer
Your City + Divorce lawyer
Your City + Law firms
Your City + Family lawyer
Your City + Business lawyer
Your City + Real estate law attorney
Your City + Personal injury attorney
Your City + Tax attorney
Your City + Auto accident lawyer
Your City + Criminal Lawyer

How to Map Out Your Website Pages for Maximum Result

Now that you are set to determine the most commonly searched keywords in your field, you can begin mapping out the pages which need to be added to your website.

Important note:

Keep in mind, each page on your website can only be optimized for 1-2 keyword combinations. If you came up with 25 keywords, then you are going to need at least 12 – 15 landing pages.

Be sure you have each keyword mapped to a specific page on your site.

Keyword	Mapped to what page
Main Keyword	Home
Keyword 1	Services - Keyword 1
Keyword 2	Services - Keyword 2
Keyword 3	Services - Keyword 3
Keyword 4	Services - Keyword 4
Keyword 5	Services - Keyword 5

For example, a personal injury attorney might come up with the following keywords: car accident, truck accident, boating accident, product liability, premises liability, slip-and-fall accidents

Keyword	Mapped to which page
personal injury attorney	Home Page
personal injury law firm	Home Page
personal injury attorneys	About Us Page
best personal injury attorney	Home Page
car accidents	Practice Areas Page

Now that you have mapped out the pages to be included on your website, you can start thinking about how to optimize each of those pages for the major search engines (Google, Yahoo, Bing, and DuckDuckGo).

HOW TO OPTIMIZE FOR RANKING IN THE ORGANIC LISTINGS

Step 1 – Build the website

Obtain more placeholders on the major search engines.

A typical service-oriented website has only 5-7 pages (Home – About Us – Practice Areas – Media – Testimonials - Contact Us), which does not create significant indexation or placeholders on the major search engines. Most lawyers, for example, provide a wide variety of services within the legal field, as covered in the Keyword Research section of this chapter.

However, Google Best Practices will require a significantly greater number of pages that most people don't even think about or ever see. For example, site map, location(s), privacy policy, terms of use, and a 404-error page.

By building out the website and creating separate pages highlighting each of the services offered (combined with city modifiers), a law firm can get listed on the search engines for each of those different keyword combinations.

Here is an example:

- Home – About – Media – Contact Us
- Sub-pages for each service – Personal Injury, Truck Accidents, Auto Accidents, Bike Accidents, Dog Bites, Medical Malpractice, etc.

Law firms often provide services in a large number of locations outside of their primary city. In order to be found on the major search engines for EACH of those sub-cities, additional pages need to be created:

- Sub-pages for each sub-city serviced – Personal Injury, Truck Accidents, Auto Accidents, Bike Accidents, Dog Bites, Medical Malpractice, etc.

Step 2 – Optimize Pages for Search Engines: How to Build Up Website Authority

Once you build the pages and complete the "on-page" SEO, your next step is getting inbound links to help you rank on page one for your most important keywords.

Everything we have discussed to this point laid the groundwork. The pages must be in order to even be in the running. However, it is the number of QUALITY inbound links and web references to those pages that determine placement.

Building the pages is just the beginning. The only way to get your site to rank above your competition is by having MORE quality inbound links and citations to your site.

The firm that has the MOST Quality Inbound Links- QILs has more leads and therefore more REVENUE!

If there is any secret to ranking well in the search engines, it is links and authority. The major caveat? Focus. You can't use garbage links. You don't want to have a thousand links. By links, I'm referring to other websites hyper-linking to your website, which I'll explain a bit more with specific examples.

Most of the algorithm changes are designed to prevent spam. Many internet marketers and SEO coordinators realize it's all about the links. That is what the Google algorithm was built upon. They figured out ways to get a variety of links with random anchor text pointed back to the pages they want to be ranked. Google has recognized that if those links are not relevant, they don't add any value to the Internet.

Bad or irrelevant links can actually hurt your ranking more than help it. It's about getting quality, relevant links back to your home page and subpages through content creation and strategic link-building. How and where do you get the links?

Take a look at the visual below as a point of reference. I call this my circle of linking opportunities:

1. *Association Links* – Be sure that you have a link to your site from any industry associations to which you belong (Ex. Bar Associations, Chamber of Commerce, Networking Groups, etc.).
2. *Directory Listings* – Get your site listed on as many directory type websites as possible (Martindale-Hubbell, Avvo.com, Justia.com, etc.)

3. *Create Interesting Content/Articles* – This is probably the #1 source of inbound links. For example, you can write an article about a particular area of law and push it out to thousands of people through article directory sites that may each contain a link back to a specific page on your site.
4. *Competitive Link Acquisition* – This is the process of using tools like Raven Tools, SEO Book, and others to see what links your top competitors have, and then get those same or similar links pointed back to your website.

Association Links

In the visual, I reference some of the business associations. I'm assuming you are involved in some type of association, whether it is the state, county, and local bar association, or some other group affiliation.

Visit the websites of those organizations and get listed in the member section. This will give you citations and the opportunity to link back to your website.

Directory Links

There are numerous "low-hanging fruit" links, as I like to call them, and it all starts with your online directory listings.

Some examples include Google Maps, Yahoo Local, City Search, Justia.com, Martindale-Hubbell, Lawyers.com, Avvo.com, and the list goes on. All of these online listings let you display your law firm name, address, phone number, and a link back to your website. Some of them even allow reviews.

For the most part, adding your business information to those directories is completely free of charge. You want to make sure your law firm is listed on as many of the online directory listings as possible for authoritative linking effectiveness.

They're also valuable from the Google Maps optimization perspective because they give you citations, which are vital for getting ranked on the map. An excellent way to find additional online directories to add your law firm to is to run a search in Google for "Your Law Firm Type – Business Directory" or "Your City – Law Firm Directory". This will yield an excellent list of potential directory sites to which you can add your firm. After beginning with online directory listings, look at any associations with which you're involved.

Non-Competitive Affiliated Industries and Local Businesses

You can work with colleagues that have affiliated industry types of businesses.

Communicate with affiliated law firms in your area of law and ask if they will post a link to your website on their own site and vice versa. Utilizing your resources and teaming up with relevant companies will add more authority to your domain.

Bar Association Sites

Look at the bar associations to which you belong, beginning with required bars like your national, state, and local bars, then voluntary bar associations.

Social Media Profile Links

The other "low-hanging fruit" links are social media profiles. I devoted an entire chapter to the power of social media and how you can harness it to get repeat and referral business.

Simply from a link-building perspective, you should set up a Facebook page, Twitter account, LinkedIn profile, and YouTube channel, and place a link to each on your website. All of them allow you to enter your company's name, address, phone number, description, and, of course, a place to put your website address.

Local Association

Other local associations that you're involved in. If you're a member of the Chamber of Commerce, a networking group like BNI (Business Networking International), or if you're involved with a local charity, find out if they list their members on their websites. Another great place to get links is by typing in your city directory.

Make sure to "link" to community and legal entities that give your clients support in their process. Your willingness to enable your client's success throughout the litigation process creates a bond that pays beyond the moment the case closes.

You might be surprised at your results when you tackle these elements. You will most likely notice that you've probably got enough links to outrank your competition in your area.

Competitive Link Acquisition - CLA

I want to share some additional thoughts and strategies on how you can accomplish even more from a link-building perspective. A powerful strategy you can implement is Competitive Link Acquisition (CLA).

Here's how I think of **CLA**: If quantity inbound links are the secret sauce to outranking your competition, and if we could figure out who's linking to your competition or what links your competition has, and we can get those same or similar links pointed back to your website, then you can outrank them. Why? Because at that point you'll have more **authority**.

Competitive link acquisition is the process of figuring out who is in the top position for your most important keywords, reverse engineering their link profile to see what links they have, and getting those same or similar links pointed back to your website. A simple way to do this is to go to Google.com and type in "your city + your service" to find out who is in the top few positions.

Let's take a look at the number one placeholder. That firm holds the number one spot because that website is optimized well and Google knows the firm should be ranked well based on the quality and quantity of inbound links compared to the competition.

Once you know who this entity is, you can use a couple of different tools such as Raven Tools, Majestic SEO, Back Link Watch, etc., take their URL, input it into your tool of choice, run the report, and get a list of links in return.

So, your number one competitor is competitor.com. Google spits out a list showing they have 392 inbound links.

- This business has a link from the local Chamber of Commerce
- This business has a link from an article that he posted in the local newspaper
- This business has a link from the local networking chapter

By analyzing the types of links a successful firm has, you can systematically mimic those links and get them pointed back to your website.

Don't just do this for your first competitor, but also for your second and third, and fourth and fifth competitors. By engaging in this tactic on a consistent basis, you can start to dominate the search engines for your most important keywords.

If you build out your site for your legal services and sub-services, optimize the pages using SEO best practices, and then obtain inbound links, you will start to DOMINATE the search engines for your legal service-related keywords in your area.

RANKING your law firm will increase qualified leads, qualified conversions, and your profits!

CONTENT MARKETING STRATEGIES FOR MAINTAINING RELEVANCE

Another highly important factor in SEO is maintaining relevance in your market by adding ongoing relevant updates to your website. In the Internet Age, **content is king.**

Google Loves Fresh Content!

With the changes in the Google algorithm, you may get discounted if they're not seeing fresh information posted on a consistent basis, even if you've got a great website with the right title tags and all the best links.

Google loves fresh content; therefore, it is vital to implement a methodology where you are creating and posting content to your website on a regular basis. Here is a framework for figuring out what kind of content you could write, why you should create content, and how to do it consistently.

First, understand and accept that you are a subject matter expert in your area of law. You might not consider yourself a writer or a content creator, but you are a subject matter expert.

You know things that the general population does not. You're an authority when it comes to the legal services you offer, with a team of people who are also proficient in this area. Create the content on the topics you know most about.

You can write about a variety of different topics, including one or two relevant keywords. You may not realize it at first, but there are innumerable subjects in your industry for which you can create content. For best results, blogs must be between 800-1,000 words.

Types of Content

Content is not limited to written words; it can take a variety of forms. The most popular content includes articles, photos, videos, and audio files. Stop and think about what content creation method works best for you.

Some people's strength is the ability to write well. Others, like me, prefer to create videos because we're comfortable in front of a camera. The point is that you can create content in multiple ways. Because I enjoy it, I'll use video as an example. A lawyer can set up a camera and record himself explaining the practice areas his firm focuses on in the market, in the same manner he would explain it to a client.

From that one video, you can create multiple pieces of content to upload to YouTube, Vimeo, Meta Café, etc. One piece of content can create multiple invaluable links to your website. Save the audio portion of that video and you've got an audio clip. You can upload that audio file to your website and post it on other various sites. For instance, you can use a transcription service like Castingwords.com, where you upload the audio or video file and somebody converts it to text.

For a minimal investment, you'll have a complete article comprising what you said. Now you've got a piece of content you can post to your blog. You can put it on Martindale-Hubbell or one of those other article directory sites for lawyers.

Content Consistency

You want to create content on a consistent basis, using the blog on your website as the hub, then syndicate it to various sources.

By syndicating the blog to article directory sites (in text form), and sending it to video sites like Vimeo, Metacafe, and YouTube.com (in video form), you'll keep the content fresh on your website/domain and create significant authority, which will significantly impact the overall ranking of your website on the search engines.

Be sure you're appropriating each one of these link-building opportunities to maximize your rank potential in your area. You might be surprised that the services you offer are highly competitive from an SEO perspective. Many law firms want to rank for the same keywords and have invested in the internet and ranking higher in the search engines.

Now that you've built out your website with effective content to generate leads and nurture existing clients, and have established an ongoing link-building and content development strategy, start looking at **Google Maps Optimization** and getting ranked on the Google Map.

CHAPTER SIX

Google Maps Optimization – How to Get Ranked on the Google Map in Your Area

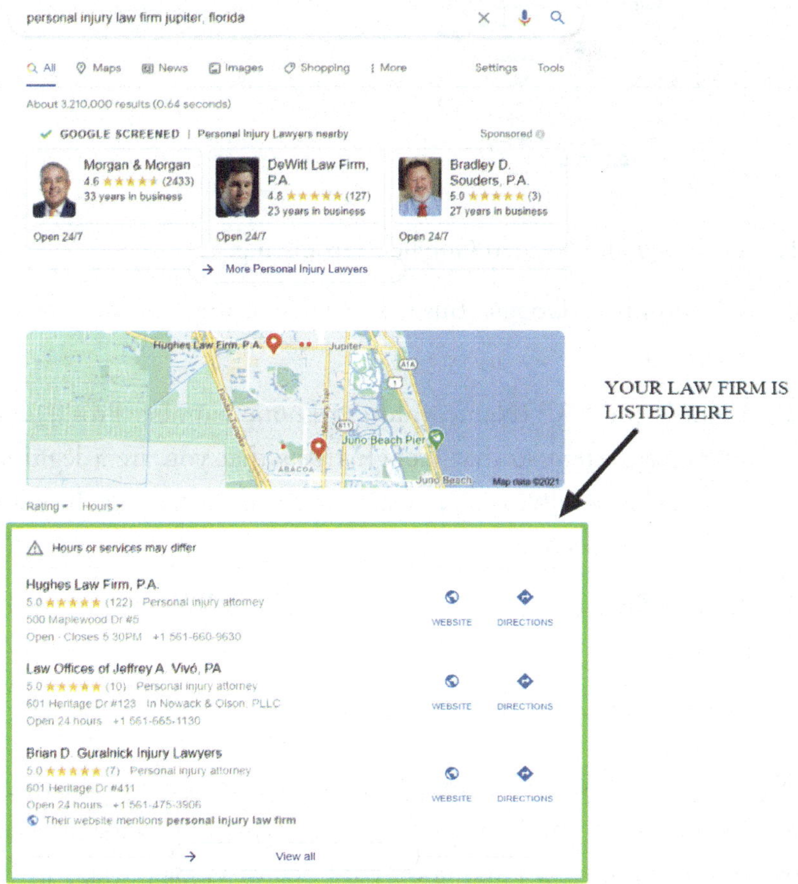

THE FUNDAMENTALS OF GOOGLE MAPS RANKING (NAP, CITATIONS, CONSISTENCY AND REVIEWS)

There are hundreds and hundreds of factors involved in getting listed on the first page of the Google Map for "Your City + Service". However, it comes down to five primary factors.

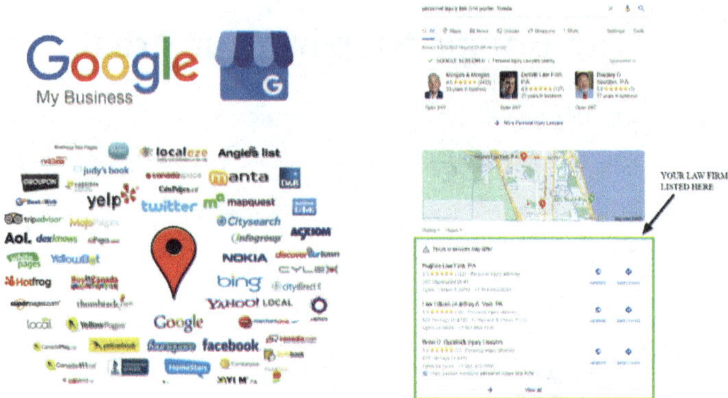

1. A claimed and verified Google Map Listing.
2. An optimized Google Business Profile listing for the area you operate in.
3. A consistent NAP (Name, Address, Phone Number Profile)in the online ecosystem so that Google trusts that you are a legitimate business located in the place you have listed and serving the market you claim to serve.
4. Website SEO that is synergistic with the Off-Website Google Best Practices.
5. Reviews from your customers in your area of law.

Depending on your market's competitiveness, if your firm implements each of these five factors as part of your marketing plan, you will significantly improve the probability of ranking on page one of Google Maps in your market.

HOW TO ESTABLISH A STRONG NAP PROFILE

Consistency is Key

As I mentioned above, a consistent Name, Address, Phone Number (NAP) profile across the web is essential for ranking well on the Google Map in your area. Google trusts you more and sees it as a signal of authority.

Rather than jumping directly into claiming your Google Map listing and citation-building, it's critical to start by determining your true NAP so that you can ensure that it is referenced consistently across the web.

What do I mean by consistency? Always reference the legitimate name for your business. For example, if your law firm's name is "ABC Personal Injury Law Group", you must always list it as "ABC Personal Injury Law Group," as opposed to just "ABC Personal Injury Law."

Be advised, misinformation abounds about how to list your law firm name online. You may read an article that suggests you keyword your name. For instance, if your name is "ABC Personal Injury Law Group," somebody might tell you it would be wise to add to the title of your company "ABC Personal Injury Law Group| Dallas Lawyer." But it is a violation of Google Business Profile policies and procedures to randomly represent your law firm using different names.

List your exact law firm name the same way across the board on all your directory sources and use the same phone number in all those places. I'm a big advocate for tracking phone numbers and what is happening with your marketing. But when it comes to your online directory listings, use your primary business phone number, the one you've been using from the beginning.

Don't try to create some unique number or a vanity number for each one of your directories. This inconsistent NAP will confuse the algorithm, creating distrust in the business listing in these directories. Google will penalize you, which impedes your ability to rank in search engines for important keyword searches.

Use your primary phone number in all those places, your exact company name, and your principal address, written the same way. If your law firm is located at "1367 South West 87th Street, Suite Number 105, " list it just like that every single time.

Don't Forget the Little Details!

Don't neglect to include the suite in one place and then put it on in another. Don't spell out "South West" in one place and put "SW" in the other. Our goal is a consistent name/address profile across the web.

A good way to figure out what Google considers to be your NAP is to run a search on Google for "Your Company" and see how it is referenced on the Google Map.

Compare that to the other high-authority sites like Martindale-Hubbell, Justia.com, Lawyers.com, and others. Look for the predominant combination of NAP, then reference it for all your directory work moving forward.

How to Properly Claim and Optimize Your Google Business Profile Listing

Below you will find a step-by-step guide for checking, claiming, and managing your Local Business Listings on Google.

1. Go to https://www.google.com/business/

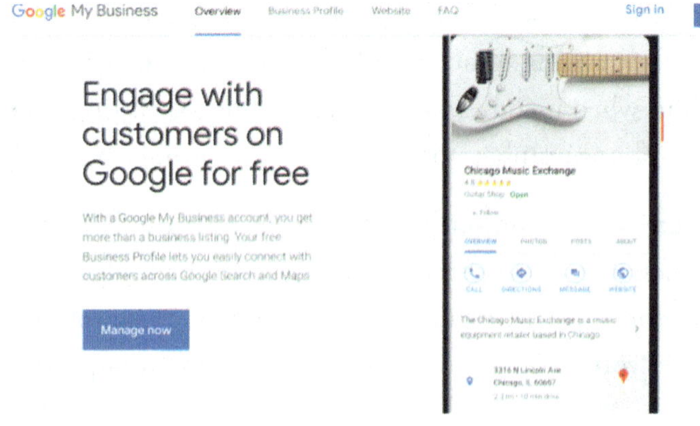

2. Create an Account and claim your business

Google My Business

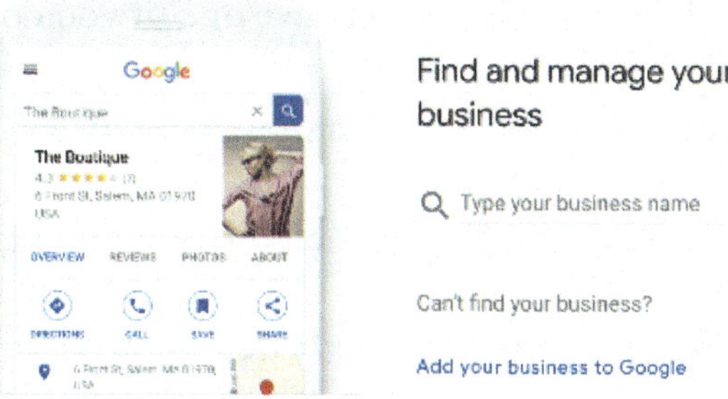

3. Enter your business address and all pertinent information
4. Choose a verification method
    - By postcard
    - By phone
    - By email
    - Instant verification
    - Bulk verification
5. Once you've created a profile, go to your Google Business Profile Dashboard and fill in all the necessary information to optimize your profile.
    - Update your company name to read "Law Firm Name" – e.g. ABC Personal Injury Law Group. Don't add any additional keywords here.
    - Add your website address to create an important inbound link.

- Upload AS MANY PHOTOS AS POSSIBLE – use personal photos, pictures of yourself (the owner), your staff, the office, your logo, your building, etc. *People connect and resonate with images. Leverage that in your Map Listing.*

- Upload a video if you have one (if you don't – make one!).

- List your hours of operation and services/practice areas.

Optimize your Google Business Profile Listing

You'll manage your business listing from your Google Business Profile Dashboard. This is where you'll make changes to your company information and gain insights into the popularity of your business by seeing how many times your profile has been viewed on Google Maps.

Be Aware of the Numerous Best Practices to properly optimize your Map listing.

- *Company Name* – Always use your legal Company Name – don't cram additional words into the name field. For example: if your company name is, "ABC Personal Injury Law Group," don't try to put additional keywords like "ABC Personal Injury Law Group – Dallas". This would violate the Google Places guidelines and reduce your probability of ranking.

- *Address* – On the "Address Field" use your EXACT legal address. Ensure that the same address is listed on your Google Places listing as on all the other online directory listings like YellowPages.com, CitySearch.com, Yelp.com, etc. The consistency of your NAP (Name, Address, Phone Number Profile) is vital for placement.

- *Phone Number* – Use a local number (not an 800 number), and make sure it is your real office number rather than a tracking number. We find that 800 numbers don't rank well. If you use a tracking number, it won't be consistent with your other online directory listings and result in poor ranking.

- *Categories* – You are allowed to select up to 10 categories. Your primary category has the greatest influence on your local rankings; therefore, must be chosen with extra care. You can edit your categories in the GBP dashboard at any time, with the understanding that doing so can substantially alter the rankings you're experiencing for various search phrases. You must choose at least one category. Do not just pick the terms "lawyer" or "law firm." Choose the more specific category, "personal injury lawyer," versus a more general category, "lawyer."

- *Service area and location settings* – Google offers two options here:

    1. No, all customers come to my location
    2. Yes, I serve customers at their location

Select Option number one.

- The next option is "Do not show my address". If you work from a home office, it is required that you select "Do not show my address." Not doing so puts you at risk of having your listing deleted.

- If you don't have a business address or a home address to list, the only other option is a virtual office. NOTE: Unfortunately, P.O. Box addresses and mailboxes don't tend to rank well.

- Picture and Video Settings – You can upload up to 500 pictures and five 30-second (max) videos. Your videos must meet the following requirements. Duration: up to 30 seconds long. File size: up to 75 MB Resolution: 720p or higher. After a video is uploaded, it can take up to 24 hours for it to be visible on the business listing.

- Use this opportunity to upload authentic content about your law firm. It's always best to use real photos of your team, office, and equipment rather than stock photos.
- Pictures – You can get more SEO value from this section by saving the images to your hard drive with a naming convention like "your city + keyword – your law firm name," rather than the standard file name. You can also create geo context for the photos by uploading them to a video sharing site like Panoramio.com (a Google Property) that enables you to Geotag your photos to your company's location.
- Videos – Upload VIDEOS. They DO NOT have to be professionally produced and will resonate well with your customers. A best practice is to upload the videos to YouTube and then Geotag them using the advanced settings.

Once you have optimized your listing using the best practices referenced above, ensure that you do not have any duplicate listings on Google Maps.

Duplicate Listings

We have found that even just one or two duplicates can prevent your listing from ranking on page one. In order to identify and merge duplicate listings, run a search on Google for "Company Name, City."

To clean up duplicates, click on the listing in question and then click "edit business details."

- Click "This is a duplicate" to let Google know that the listing should be merged with your primary listing.

If you follow these best practices, you will have a well-optimized Google Maps listing for your Business.

How to Develop Authority for your Map Listing via Citation Development

Now that you have claimed your Google Business Profile Listing and optimized it to its fullest, you must build authority.

Having a well-claimed and optimized local listing doesn't automatically rank you on page one. Google wants to list the most legitimate and qualified providers first. How do they figure out who gets the page one listings?

Well, there are a number of determining factors, but one focuses on how widely the company is referenced on various online directory sites such as Martindale-Hubbell, Avvo.com, Justia.com, and others.

Citations are web references to your business name, address, and phone number. You can add citations in a variety of ways. There are directory listings that you should claim manually and others that you can submit to via submission services like Universal Business Listing or Yext.com to save time. However, your listings within these services can often get mixed up with inaccurate information that may be in the ecosystem. Claim your listings manually to ensure that you are in control and can make updates/edits as needed.

Top Data Aggregators

Data aggregators are data mining systems that spread business information online. They collect and share business data with a multitude of sources, including search engines like Google. If your NAP is incorrect in the data aggregators, your information will be incorrect in the online ecosystem. There are four primary data aggregators:

- Infogroup
- Localeze
- Factual
- Foursquare

TOP Citation Sources to Claim Manually:

- Google Business Profile
- Bing Local
- Yahoo Local
- City Search
- Yelp
- YP.com
- Merchant Circle
- Manta

List of the Top Citation Sources for Law Firms

- Lawyers.com (http://www.lawyers.com/)
- Martindale (http://www.martindale.com/)
- Find Law (http://www.findlaw.com/)
- USLegal Lawyers (http://lawyers.uslegal.com/)
- Legal Webfinder (http://www.legalwebfinder.com/)
- List Lawyers (http://www.list-lawyers.com/)
- USA Attorneys (http://usattorneys.com/)
- HG (https://www.hg.org/)
- Attorney Directory Database (https://attorneydirectorydb.org/)
- Injury Lawyers (http://injurylawyers.jouwweb.nl/)

By securing these high-quality citations, you will boost your authority and highly improve your probability of ranking in the Google Map Listings. The next critical step is to get online reviews.

VERTICAL DIRECTORIES

A vertical directory is a website directory that focuses on a particular category of products or services. In law, there are over 153 free and paid directories as of this book's printing.

Joining legal directories is one of the simplest and most effective ways for attorneys to grow their online presence while building links at the same time. Directories like Martindale-Hubbell, FindLaw, and Lawyers.com among others, can help law firms expand their visibility in search results pages, collaborate with other professionals, get authoritative links to their site, and grow their online authority.

Why Are Legal Directories Important?

Google started de-indexing spammy directories back in 2012 and devalued links from such sites. Today, submitting your law firm website to quality legal directories is still an important part of building citations and relevant links.

How to Get Online Reviews: Real Reviews from actual clients

After you've claimed and optimized your listing, established your NAP, and developed your citations across the web, the next critical component for getting ranked on Google Maps is obtaining reviews.

- ❖ **You must have real reviews from actual clients in your true service area**

- ❖ **Authenticity is critical to establishing a bond with your clients**

KEEP IT REAL

First, do not fill the system with fake or fraudulent reviews. Do not create bogus accounts and post reviews to Google Maps, Yelp, City Search, etc. just for the sake of having reviews. That will not help you; you need real reviews from your actual clients in your geographic service area.

You might be thinking, "Why is that important?" or "How would Google know the difference?" Google pays close attention to the reviewer's profile. An active Google user with a Gmail account and a YouTube channel is typically connected to a Google profile.

Suppose that person with the active profile has had their account for seven years and happens to be located in your geographic service area. If he or she writes you a review, Google considers it credible and will count it in your favor.

Conversely, if somebody creates a Google account with the sole intent of writing a review, it obviously is not credible; Google is capable of catching on to that. That account has no associated history and originates right at your office IP address. Google will flag the review as a bogus submission.

For these reasons, you must implement an authentic strategy to connect with real people who will write your reviews. Do not play the system because Google, Yelp, and the popular online review sites are fully aware of this tactic.

Getting Reviews

That said, how can you obtain reviews? What kind of process will help you get reviews from your real clients in your geographic service area?

First, print up some review cards (I provide a sample later in this chapter). A review card is a simple document with your law firm's logo and a short and sweet thank you note, as you will see in the following image.

From: Law Offices of Paul J Burkhart, PL.
Subject: John, Would You Like A Complimentary Starbucks Gift Card from Law Offices of Paul J Burkhart, PL.?

Dear John Smith,

You are the reason Law Offices of Paul J Burkhart, PL. exists! We strive to be the best we can. Hearing from you would be incredibly valuable to us. Would you kindly take 45 seconds and give us your feedback using the following link?

Click Here to Share Your Review

As a token of our appreciation you will receive a free Starbucks Gift Card valued at $10.00.

Thank you again for your time in advance and trusting us with your business.

Best Regards,
The team at,
Law Offices of Paul J Burkhart, PL.

Unsubscribe

"Thanks so much for your business. We appreciate the opportunity to serve you. We'd love it if you would write us a review." Then provide a link to a page on your website where they can write the review.

Do some homework on the front end and provide a page on your website exclusively for reviews: yourlawfirm.com/reviews. On that page, display links to the various places where people can write your reviews.

Include a link to your Google Maps listing, Yahoo local listing, Lawyers.com or Avvo.com listing, CitySearch listing, and any others.

Why provide a variety of options for posting reviews? Two reasons:

1. You want a significant number of reviews on Google maps. But Google also looks at your reviews on other websites like Yelp, Lawyers.com, and other pages.

2. You must diversify where your clients post reviews. It appears more authentic to have 12 on Google and 17 on Lawyers.com than 72 reviews on Google maps.

Industry experts recommend having at least 10 reviews across 10 different review sites/directories while you continue to generate fresh reviews over time.

Make it Easy

Make it as easy as possible for your clients to post reviews. Remember, different people use different systems. Personally, I'm a big Google user. If you sent me an email or gave me a card that requested a review and provided various options, I'm going to click on Google and write my review.

On the other hand, some people don't have Google accounts. However, they may rely on other directories like Lawyers.com or use Yelp more often to post reviews of businesses they've used.

They have active accounts somewhere and it would be much easier for them to write the reviews there. The easier and more convenient you make it for your clients, the better their response.

As we mentioned, Google looks at the reviewer's profile. If you only give them one option -- the Google Map -- but they happen to be a Yelp user without a Google account, they will have to go out of their way to create an account to write the review.

This is not likely to happen, but for the sake of argument, let's assume they decided to create an account. Their review won't count for much because there's no active profile.

By providing options, the Yelp user that has a reputation for writing reviews will make a difference when they write one for you. It will stick as opposed to being filtered. Make it easy for your clients to choose the most convenient option for them.

NOW LET'S GET BACK TO THE STRATEGY

Phase one, print out review cards. Ask your staff (administrator or receptionist) to hand them out after a client visits. The card can read something like: "Thanks for giving us the opportunity to assist you with your legal needs. We appreciate your business. I just want to leave this with you. If you'd be willing to write us a review and share your experience, we would really appreciate it."

You're showing appreciation and holding yourself accountable by asking for feedback. When you do that consistently, you will encourage clients to share your firm's name.

Next, develop an email list of your **circle of influence** to boost your amount of reviews. Your circle of influence includes **your most recent clients**, the ones who have been using your services for quite some time. Compile a list of clients who would be willing to act on your behalf.

Put the email list – whether it's 10 contacts or 700 contacts – in an Excel sheet. Include their names and email addresses. Then, use a tool like Constant Contact or MailChimp to send an email blast with the following message:

> **Email Subject: Thanks for hiring our firm. (Name of firm)**
>
> Name,
> I wanted to send you a quick email to thank you for your business and let you know how much we appreciate the opportunity to serve you.

Our goal is to provide 100 percent satisfaction for our clients and exceed your expectations every step of the way. I certainly hope that we did just that.

If so, it would help us out if you'd be willing to post a review for us online at one of your favorite online review sites. Below are a few samples of direct links where you could write a public review about your experience with us:

- Google - https://support.google.com/maps/answer/6230175?co=GENIE.Platform%3DDesktop&hl=en
- Yelp - https://www.yelp.com/writeareview

Thank you again!

Warm regards,

(Your name) Law Firm

Again, save them the time of finding the websites on their own by providing some links to the various places where they can write reviews. An email like this will create an uptick in your online review profiles. And as I have mentioned repeatedly, reviews are crucial.

Getting 10 reviews on Google Maps is essential to dominating the digital space.

Reviews make a direct impact on how you rank on Google, which in turn creates a perception about your firm in the minds of consumers who are looking for a reputable attorney or law firm. Your goal is to move beyond that 10-review threshold as quickly as possible.

This will help you obtain real reviews from real people that have real online profiles. Implement a system in which you ask for reviews on a consistent basis from the clients you represent. The best way to do that is to **request an email address from your customers at the point of service.**

At Law Firm Marketing Pros, we have developed a robust review getting system called Top-Rated Law Firm that automates and simplifies the process.

Establishing Your Email Database

In our experience, clients are more apt to respond to review requests when they have had a win in their case – this does not necessarily mean that they won the case, but that something positive has happened.

That's how you start to develop a database of emails. We are going to talk about email marketing later in the book as part of your online marketing plan, but for this purpose, you need an email address so that you can send a message after service thanking them for their business and asking them to write you a review.

Your amount of reviews from actual clients will increase exponentially if you repeat this process regularly. This is how you can start to dominate the Google Map, because reviews and citations work in harmony for ranking.

Sample 'Review Us' Landing Page for your Website

Law Firm
MARKETING PROS
MORE LEADS · MORE CLIENTS · MORE PROFITS

Jupiter

Rating

★★★★★

Comments 0

Name

Email

Rate Us!

By sharing this data, you authorize its use per our Terms of Use.
To withdraw or limit consent please contact us.

If you follow these steps to properly claim your Google Map listing, develop your authority via citation development, and put a systematic process in place to get real reviews from your real clients in your true service area, you will be well on your way to dominating the Google Map listings in your market.

Dominating GOOGLE MAPS listings is essential to your firm's success online.

CHAPTER SEVEN

Website Conversion Fundamentals – How to Ensure That Your Website Converts Visitors into Leads in the Form of Calls and Web Submissions

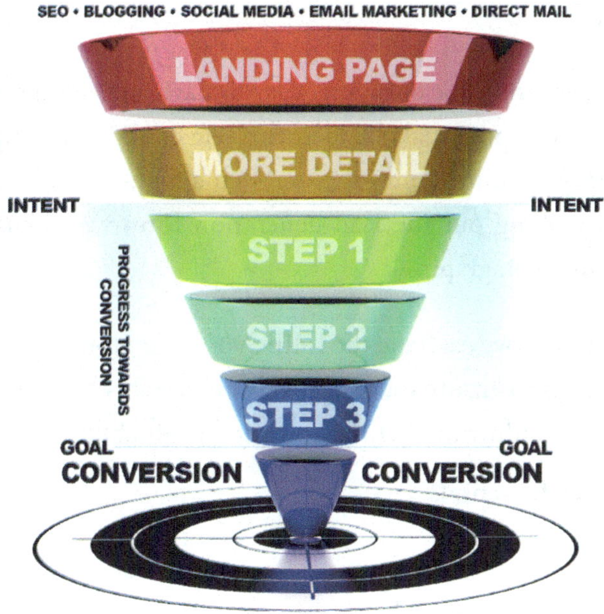

If you're going to invest your hard-earned money in digital marketing, you must convert the traffic to your website into action. At a basic level, your website's purpose is to compel your potential clients to take the action you want them to take; for example, "call for a consultation" or fill out a lead generation form. According to Crazy Egg, five years ago, 50% of all website traffic took some action when they got to your website. As of 2017, it was 1.6%.

In this chapter, we'll discuss how to set up your website, what type of messaging to include, and your website's navigational flow to ensure maximum conversion and profitability from your entire online marketing effort.

You can have the best pay-per-click campaign, search engine optimization, and a number one ranking on Google Maps. However, if your website's content and structure are not compelling for users, they have no reason to choose you over the competition. Your website doesn't give them the information they need to easily conclude, "You're the law firm I am going to call for help."

Your firm's website must be engaging, easy to navigate, and understandable enough to keep your potential clients there long enough to compel them to take the action you want them to take. Such actions include calling for a consultation or filling out the lead generation form we discussed in this chapter's opening paragraph.

Let's talk about how we can take the traffic you'll get from organic and pay-per-click strategies to ensure that your website presents the correct message to maximize your online marketing strategies' profitability and revenue.

Conversion Fundamentals

Be real. I talked about how consumers react more positively to authentic interactions with real people. They like to see the law firm, the people they will speak with on the phone, and the people who will provide critical legal advice – and sometimes manage life-changing situations on their behalf. For this reason, avoid stock photography as much as you can.

Provide photos of the firm's staff, the office, and the kind of environment your firm wants to project based on the area of law you practice and the clients you want to attract.

Having a sense of the law firm and the environment makes clients feel more comfortable, which creates trust and lets them know they will be working with real people. *In the field of law, especially, clients want to know who will be handling their case.*

As networking and referral expert Bob Burg says, *"All things being equal, people do business with people they* ***know, like and trust.****"*

Your website's content and messaging must draw them in and inform them to help them connect with your firm's mission. Because they're looking for a reputable, well-established law firm, when they land on your homepage, the first message your potential clients see should enforce the fact that they can trust you.

Write something along the lines of, "Are you looking for a law firm you can trust? Then you've come to the right place. We're operating on the same principles for the last 30 years: trust, innovation, and excellence."

Connect with them. Give your website visitors reasons to choose you and provide a call to action: "Give us a call at this number for immediate service," or, "Click here to find out if our firm is best suited to your legal needs." Remember, they've browsed around the internet and know that there are hundreds of law firms from which they can choose.

Give these potential clients relevant information about who you are and why they want to choose you. Ask them to call now for a consultation (if you offer free consultations, say "free consultations") to incentivize them to select you and make that call right away.

What to Write

When it comes to the copy on your website, you must address their specific concerns. For example, if you own a law firm, on the homepage, write something generic, "Looking for a trusted law firm?" On the divorce attorney page, sympathize with them. "I know how frustrating it is when you filed for divorce and the process is not meeting your expectations. You must ensure that you've got the right team on your side – proven lawyers who have successfully navigated the family law system with positive out-comes for their clients."

Write that kind of messaging for each one of your website pages, including a clear call to action after every block of text urging them to "Call now to schedule your consultation" or "Find out how much my case is worth."

Create more robust engagement on your website by adding "About Us" links, success stories, testimonials, useful resources, and videos. Give them content that makes them think, "These guys know what they're doing," and draws them more deeply into the website, so they're more inclined to take the next step. Tell them why they should select your firm over the competition.

You should, of course, provide a lead generation form (you may know it as a comment or question box) on each page of your website. If you can afford it, offer a live chat option, too. A live chat option is imperative because not everyone is ready to pick up the phone and talk to a lawyer or paralegal. Since you don't want to lose them, this gives them the option to type in their name, email address, and phone number and let you contact them. Again, make sure your phone number appears on the top right-hand corner and that there is a clear call to action on every page of your website, under every block of text:

Check out our reviews, look at our firm's credentials

Explain why they should hire you. Leverage personality. Be authentic. Integrate your photos into your website. This content will be critical to conversion. There are multiple websites with slick images. Consumers aren't drawn into those images unless they feel real and make a connection with them.

Utilize your reviews, testimonials, and videos. Create a simple video for each of the pages on your website, explaining your practice areas and why your firm is the best. Some people are visual: they can see the content on the website, read it, and feel fine. Other people are more auditory and would prefer to hear the message.

If you can spend the time to provide both text and video, it significantly impacts conversion. Give them external proof. Take them out to the review sites to preview testimonials on FindLaw, Lawyers.com, Google Business Profile, etc. Show them what other people are saying to improve your conversion dramatically.

Example of a Law Firm Website that is Built to Convert

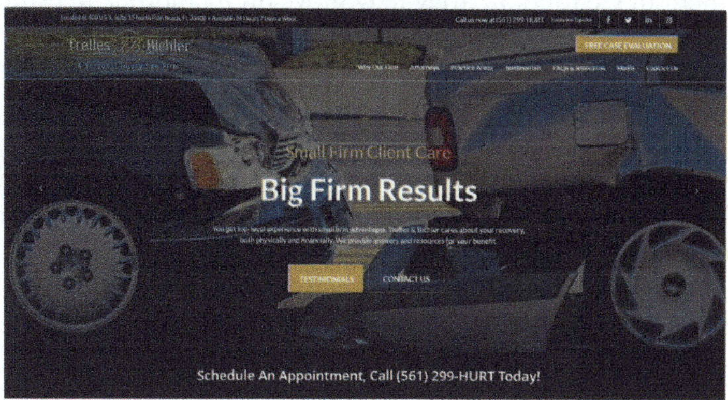

Internet marketing involves many little things performed in sequence to compel people to call your law firm when they require your service. That is why it is essential not to break convention. Don't get cute and try to do something different because you may confuse your potential clients and bounce them off your website. Always remember, they are one or two clicks of the back button away from your competitor.

In his book, *Marketing Myopia*, Theodore Levitt discusses how business owners get too narrowly focused on themselves. Attorneys tend to be particularly guilty of this. It should not be about you; it should be about them - your potential clients. Always follow website design conventions, which include:

1. The company logo should always be on the top left-hand side of the page. Their logo here is a perfect size. Sometimes clients tell me they want their logo to be triple this size. The reality is that few searchers know you from your company name, so occupying too much space with just your logo is a waste of valuable webpage real estate.

2. Your phone number is VITAL for the credibility of your company. It should be as close to the top right-hand corner as possible. Make sure it's large and easy to find. Try not to make people search for it. It's frustrating for searchers, and you have just a few seconds for them to see it before they may move on to another website. People always look to the top of the page for that vital piece of information.

3. Professionally shot photos. For a small investment, you could and should hire a professional photographer to come in and take pictures. You will use them everywhere. DIY photography is okay, but a professional photo is much better.

4. A small blurb of text confirming you have been in the community for X number of years and are a family-owned and operated law firm brings it all together. *People buy from people, not hidden companies* (law firms). Personalize your website as much as possible. Your website is a marketing tool, and its job is to lead capture and eliminate as many buying barriers as possible.

Main navigation. Your website's main navigation should be easy to find, and the links should be descriptive. Give people the option of moving around your website. One of Google's algorithms is how many pages a person visits and what their visit length was. Guide them down a path without confusing them. In other words, give them all the information they need in as few clicks as possible, but provide them the option of navigating around your site.

1. Some people want a way to contact you without calling. For example, they might be searching at three o'clock in the morning. A contact form above the fold (the top half of the page) is excellent for capturing clients' info. You should get a lot of form submissions regularly by doing this. Without the form, you risk potential clients not taking action. Furthermore, the form is also an excellent tool for building future email marketing campaigns, designed to nurture people who are not ready to hire you yet.

2. Get to the point right away without going into too much detail. The first paragraph of your text should give you a brief introduction of who you are and what you do. You can go into further detail on your About Us page.

3. You can't see it here, but this area is a slider graphic with three images – a nice visual effect that adds movement to the page. It

also delivers three critical messages you want people to know: testimonials, contact us, and schedule an appointment.

Social media icons are great because they allow potential visitors to see another side of your law firm. It's an excellent place to publish more videos and photos and to see how your law firm interacts with its community. From an SEO point of view, it helps build your company's social signal, to which Google pays close attention. Social media is no longer just sexy "marketing speak"; it is a must for online marketing.

Don't forget about going mobile. Depending on the type of law you practice, mobile search will be greater than desktop search. Mobile search is only going to continue to grow. The critical thing with mobile is to make it easy and put all vital information front and center. Make sure everything is only a click away, and always have your 'call us' button on top.

WEBSITE CONVERSION FACTOR ANALYSIS

I have summarized the website's positive and negative points that can affect the User-Friendly Interface of the website and the website conversions.

Homepage Banners

First, "Above the Fold" should be optimized appropriately. Above-the-fold areas are the sections of the webpage that are visible without the need for scrolling. This space is critical regarding user engagement, and as such, you ought to showcase the most appealing attributes in this section. Some of the most vital conversion factors that should be present in the above-the-fold area are the following:

- ✔ Attention-grabbing headlines
- ✔ Bullet points
- ✔ Calls to Action

Form to capture leads

Please check the following Above the Fold banner for a reference:

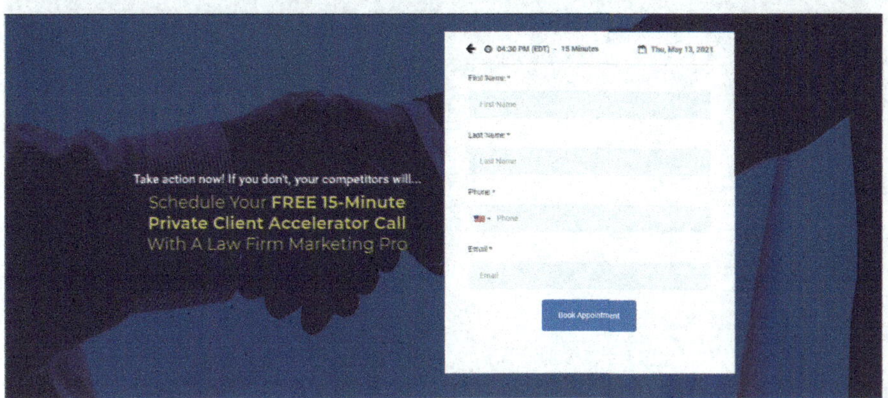

Second, you must include a proper section for "User Engagement" in the "above the fold" section of the website.

Ideally, there should be a downloadable FREE report or guide with an interesting title and a "Download Now" button in the header section. The user can download the same if they input their name and email address. Please refer to the image above.

LAW FIRM PROFILE

The homepage must have a 60% law firm focus and a 40% practice area focus.

Firm credibility is the key to user engagement, and any user must feel secure about the law firm before moving forward with browsing through the product section.

Therefore, it is crucial to have a brief law firm profile on your homepage to let users know about "who you are," "why you are different," and "what your practice areas are." We often refer to this as "Why Choose Us?"

Ideally, the homepage should contain a brief overview of the law firm and a couple of bullets describing its salient features. Please check the following example for reference:

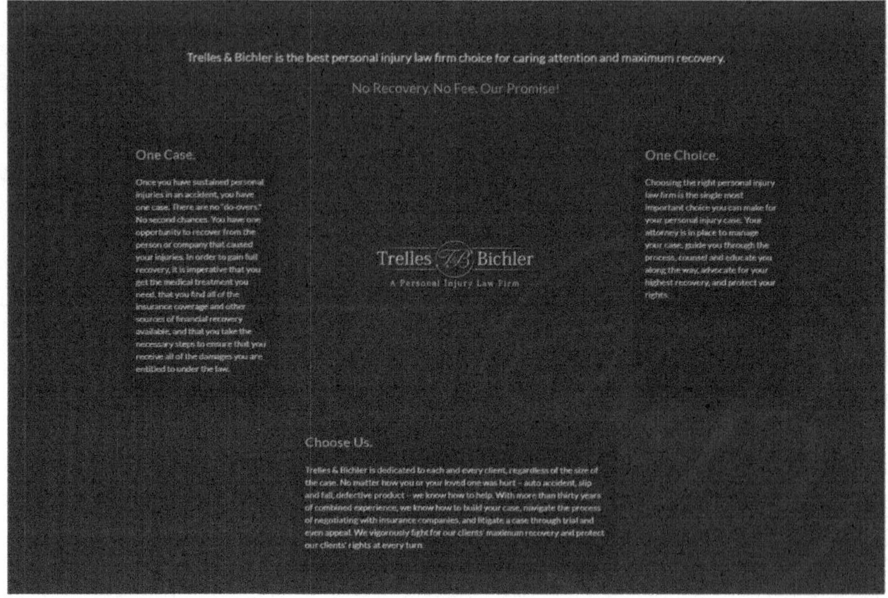

LATEST NEWS

There should be an enticing Latest News section in the main navigation, and maybe on the homepage in a professional press release format. Search engines give preference to sites that have press releases rather than articles on their homepage.

The Press Release section should have at least two latest news, with a couple of lines about the news and a visible **Read More** button. Please check the following reference.

Law Firm Marketing Pros Win Fastest-Growing Agency Award

by Daria DiGiovanni | Apr 16, 2021 | Press Releases

Josh Konigsberg and Andy Leonard, Co-Founders and Partners of Law Firm Marketing Pros, received the Fastest-Growing Agency Award among 180 agency members, from the prestigious Seven Figure Agency, a digital marketing agency mastermind group founded by digital...

Law Firm Marketing Pros Earns 2021 Impact Company of the Year Award

by Daria DiGiovanni | Mar 31, 2021 | Press Releases

DotCom Magazine announces that Law Firm Marketing Pros has been selected to join its annual Impact Company of The Year List For 2021. The DotCom Magazine Impact Company of The Year 2021 Award celebrates the most important segment of the economy – America's...

Law Firm Marketing Leader Josh Konigsberg Interviewed by DotCom Magazine for Entrepreneur Spotlight Series.

by Daria DiGiovanni | Mar 15, 2021 | Press Releases

Josh Konigsberg, a leading law firm marketing expert and influential Managing Partner of Law Firm Marketing Pros, was interviewed by DotCom Magazine as part of the online magazine's Entrepreneur Spotlight Interview Series. Konigsberg joins other leading CEOs,...

Law Firm Marketing Pros Announces Five Clients Named to 2020 Law Firm 500 List

by Daria DiGiovanni | Jan 9, 2021 | Press Releases

On Saturday, December 5, 2020, the Law Firm 500 Award committee announced the list of 2020 Honorees, including five firms that are Law Firm Marketing Pros clients, of which 2 were in the top 5 and all 5 in the top 53. They include Greathouse Trial Law (1), Atlanta...

BLOG

A blog is useful as it gives the visitors helpful information and gives credibility to the law firm. The visitor perceives that the firm is up to date with the industry's happenings.

In a post-COVID world, clients want to have a sense that your firm is up to date with any changes in laws or regulations. Make sure your firm highlights those changes to make your clients feel informed. You can use a blog in this way to connect directly with them.

With the recent algorithm changes, updating the homepage content regularly is essential in getting higher rankings on the Search Engine Results Page.

This is why the website should have a blog section on the homepage, similar to the following, and you should update the blogs regularly. Please check the following reference:

TESTIMONIALS

Positive, recent testimonials are vital since they earn credibility from your clients. Put the total number of reviews at the bottom of the review section if you have more reviews than most of your competitors.

The testimonials on your homepage should have a "Read More" which will redirect to the testimonial page. Additionally, provide multiple ways to navigate to see reviews. There are a plethora of review systems on the market today. At Law Firm Marketing Pros, we offer a robust review, acquisition, monitoring, and syndication system called Top-Rated Law Firm. Please check the following reference:

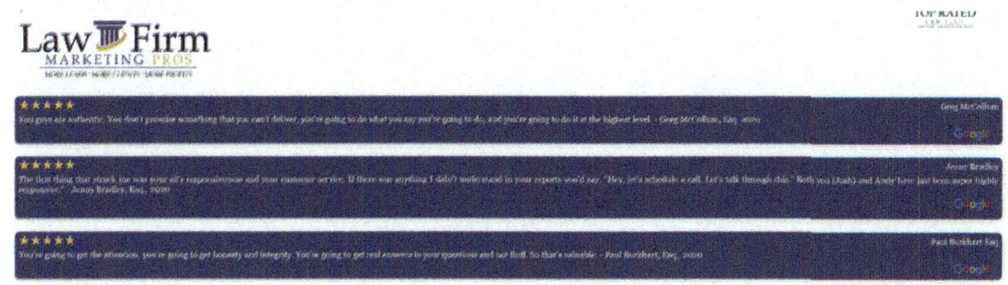

9 Reviews

Powered by Law Firm Marketing Pros

Disclosure

CHAPTER EIGHT

Mobile Optimization – How to Optimize Your Website for Mobile Visitors

More than 50 percent of mobile searches are for local businesses. You are a local business. Therefore, a significant amount of your potential clients are searching for you via a mobile device, which means you must be mobile-friendly. Here are just a few eye-opening mobile stats you should be aware of:

- Up to 70% of web traffic happens on a mobile device (Tech Jury, 2021)

- 90% of users used a mobile device to search the internet in 2020 (Statista.com)

- By 2020, the number of smartphone users is projected to reach 2.87 billion. (Review42.com)

- The World Advertising Research Center (WARC) predicts that by 2025, three-quarters (¾) of users will access the Internet using a mobile device.

- More than one-quarter of all emails are opened on smartphones. (Source: Email Monday, 2021)

- 40% of mobile users search for local businesses and often include the phrase "near me". (Source: Quora Creative)

- It is predicted that mobile ad spend will surpass 240 billion dollars by 2022. (Source: Statista.com)

- 75% of users will have a more positive opinion about your business if you have a good responsive website. (Source: Sweor.com, 2021)

- 57% of users say they wouldn't recommend a company if their mobile website design is bad. (Sweor.com, 2021)

- By 2021, 54% of all eCommerce sales will be mobile sales. (Source: BigCommerce.com)

- According to BrizFeel.com, 49% of users use their mobile devices for shopping.

- 50% of B2B search queries today are made on smartphones and grew 70% in 2020 (Google)

- 98.3% of Facebook users access the app via a mobile device (Statista, 2021)

For you, as a law firm owner, mobile access provides a unique opportunity to connect with local customers via their mobile devices. A mobile-responsive website is one that directs leads to your firm.

Before you start to develop a mobile arsenal to drive more inbound calls, you must first determine who your mobile competitors are. When you know who you're up against in mobile marketing, you can plan your strategies accordingly. To do this well, you must identify your closest competitors and the mobile techniques they use to generate their sales.

MOBILE-OPTIMIZED WEBSITES

First, to determine if your website or any website is mobile-optimized, you can easily use Google's mobile-friendly website test tool called "Mobile-Friendly Test" https://search.google.com/test/mobile-friendly. Copy the web address and paste it into the link.

Consider the following criteria:

- Did it load quickly?
- Was it easy to find their contact information and other details that consumers tend to look for while on the go?
- Was it optimized to fit your phone screen?

If so, they have invested in their business by taking care of their mobile clients and prospects.

Next, pull up your website on your mobile phone. If accessing your firm's website is a nightmare, your phone is not the problem; your website is. Consequently, you have been losing potential business.

Analyze Your Current Mobile Marketing Status

What is your status when it comes to staying connected with local consumers using Mobile Marketing strategies?

Researching your competition is a necessary task if your goal is to become the local authority in your niche. But it is equally important to analyze where your business stands now in order to move forward.

Are you running a mobile marketing campaign, but not seeing your desired results? Or do you want to start a mobile marketing campaign but keep putting it off because you don't know where to begin?

Every law firm in your local area is in a crucial fight for more clients and profits. If you want to enjoy a significant increase in your number of cases, your firm can no longer ignore the profitability of ramping up your mobile efforts.

Analyze Your Mobile Status

Many business owners spend a significant amount of money competing with similar businesses while neglecting to analyze what they themselves are doing. Analyzing your mobile status will help you identify the weaknesses that hold you back, along with the strengths that can help you gain online dominance.

You must understand where your past efforts have taken you and what your future has in store for you based on where you stand today. For starters, it is crucial that you take note of what you are and aren't doing to generate more sales using mobile marketing.

Ask yourself the following:

- Is my mobile website user-friendly? Does it load within seconds or take forever to render properly? Does my mobile website contain all the relevant information consumers look for while on the go?

- Does my mobile website show up high in the rankings on mobile search engines, or is it nowhere to be found when local consumers perform a search for my "service + your city" on their mobile devices?

- Is my opt-in/call-to-action on ALL of your printed and web marketing materials?

- Is my live chat mobile-friendly?

As you can see, there is much to consider when it comes to making sure your law firm is on the right track toward beating your local competition with mobile marketing.

Positioning Your Firm by Watching How Your Mobile Marketing Competitors Use the Platform

Do you want to know how your closest competitors are driving more business via mobile marketing? Just take a look at their campaign yourself.

Mobile marketing has recently opened new doors for businesses that want to market their products and services by using mobile phones as personal "mini billboards." The fact that more consumers rely on their mobile devices to complete their personal and business tasks supports this strategy. In fact, your clients often use their cell phones to locate and choose local products, services, and businesses every day.

To beat your competitors in the world of mobile marketing, you must know what they are doing. Digital technology is not expected to slow down anytime soon. If anything, current events have made it almost imperative for consumers to use their cell phones as main points of contact across all aspects of their lives. Your firm does not want to be left behind when it comes to leveraging advanced technology as a central part of your overall marketing tool kit.

Reviewing your competitors' mobile marketing initiatives may seem like a daunting task, but it's not. Simply identify which competitors are taking most of your clients and let the research begin.

You should begin by visiting their mobile websites on your phone. Go through the websites and take note of the look and feel, the features and the traffic flow. Although your goal is NOT to copy exactly what they're doing, you could get a few pointers for your own mobile website.

Use the information you gain from your research solely to set up a mobile marketing campaign that not only beats your competitors but also attracts new customers and instills loyalty to your firm.

YOUR FIRM APP

Mobile applications (apps) offer another excellent option for marketing your firm. I recommend Your Firm App, https://yourfirmapp.com:

"Your Firm App was founded by attorney Chris Smith with a mission to create a mobile app platform which would improve attorney-client communication by providing clients mobile access to the information they want most often.

"Recognizing the lack of cost-effective client-facing app options for his own practice, Chris began development of what has become the Your Firm App platform in 2017. Along the way, Chris has enjoyed the support of his wife Marissa who has been a co-founder in every way as they have worked to build a tech company in Oklahoma City, Oklahoma.

"The story of Your Firm App demonstrates the opportunity for anyone who sees a need in their own life and is just stubborn enough to build a solution, and evidence of the best being yet to come."

Another marketing tool you can easily investigate is your competitors' mobile applications. Download their apps to see what they're offering and to discover the user-friendliness of the applications (APPS).

Make Customers Call Your Business with Mobile Marketing

The secret to beating your competitors in the business is making your law firm more interesting to your target client. There are several ways to do this using mobile marketing if you: **plan ahead**, **focus on the right elements of the mobile marketing methods**, and **maintain your campaigns over time.**

As much as you would like to boot your local competitors out of the picture, the fact is a lot of them will probably be using some of the same mobile marketing methods as you.

That is why your main focus should be compelling your potential clients to choose your law firm over theirs, which is fairly easy to do with consistent and persistent effort.

It is up to you which tools you employ to attract new clients and maintain relationships with your existing clients

Here are a few tips which can work in your favor and help local consumers choose you:

- A good, mobile-friendly website that is easily accessible by mobile phone users in your area. People use their mobile phones to search the web for local products and services while on the go. Make sure your site loads quickly, provides the precise information they need, and is easy to navigate.

- If you choose to start a text message marketing campaign, your text messages must be short and informative, offer great value, and relay a clear message. Send messages out consistently, yet conservatively. Create a careful balance that makes sense for your business and target audience. Need a boost in getting new mobile subscribers? Give your clients and prospects a compelling incentive in exchange for opting in. Then, watch your list grow exponentially.

- Consumers love businesses that are savvy about digital media.
- Consumers expect you to have a website, an active presence on their favorite social media outlets, and to access your firm easily from their mobile devices.
- Your marketing plan may include a mobile app developed to aid in keeping your local consumers connected with your business.
- Implement the use of QR codes as a way to keep your local consumers engaged and provide them with "instant gratification." The key to having a client choose your firm over the others is the ease of access first!
- Mobile SEO should be used well to attract qualified traffic to your website. Mobile users search for local products and services constantly on their mobile devices when out and about. If your law firm does not rank in the results, there is a major potential for loss of profits due to clients choosing another firm based on their GOOGLE ranking.

Finding Your Basics

If somebody goes online, searches for your legal services, and lands on your website, they probably want basic information. Most likely, they are not interested in gathering a ton of information about you; they simply want to know who you are, where you're located, your practice areas, and then press a button to chat with a lawyer or a staff member who can set up a consultation.

The example below features a mobile version of a site where prospects can obtain basic information, click the "Book an Appointment" button, and schedule an appointment. Set up a mobile version of your site, provide the fundamental information, and don't overcomplicate it.

Get More Leads Now

Full Name (required)

Full Name

Firm Name (required) *

Enter your Firm Name

Mobile Number (required) *

Enter your phone number

Your Email (required) *

Enter your email address

Your Information Is Safe With Us

Get Started

Now that you have your website conversion fundamentals in order and have a proactive Mobile Marketing plan, you can start to think about Social Media Marketing.

Law firms throughout the country are already using this technology to expand their client base. You can place your firm at the top of the list by utilizing all of the marketing tools at your disposal. Mobile Marketing is a critical piece of an effective plan.

CHAPTER NINE

Social Media Marketing – How to Leverage Social Media (Facebook, Twitter, Instagram & Other Social Platforms) for Maximum Effect in Your Business

Social media (Facebook, Twitter, YouTube, Instagram) is omnipresent in our society, but can a business leverage it? How can you use social media to grow your law firm?

By now, I hope you've learned how to position your law firm online, and rank well on the organic listings on Google Maps and in the organic non-paid listings. Now, it's time to focus on social media marketing, and the many ways in which you can utilize social media platforms like Facebook, Twitter, and Instagram to grow your law firm.

As I talk to attorneys throughout the country about internet marketing and social media, I usually see puzzled expressions on their faces. The most frequent question they ask is, "How in the world does all of this social media stuff apply to my law firm? How can I possibly use Facebook in a way that would help me increase my revenues, boost client inquiries, and get more cases?"

Let's bridge the gap on where the "lowest-hanging fruit" for social media is in your firm by posing a different question: "What's your number one source of cases and clients today?"

SPHERE OF INFLUENCE

I'm sure you have already considered the question and arrived at the conclusion that repeated and referral business is your number one source of revenue.

Your reputation and the things your clients say about your law firm after you've handled their case is the lifeblood of any law firm. A critical factor in the client-building process obtaining referrals from your existing clients.

When you harness the power of social media correctly, it enables you to take that repeat and referral business and build on them exponentially.

Why do I tout social media as an excellent place to connect with your clients and get more repeat and referral business? Check out these important statistics from Sprout Social and HootSuite from the year 2020:

- Facebook currently has 2.28 billion monthly active users in the U.S.
- The average Facebook user has 338 friends
- Facebook users check in an average of 14 times per day
- Instagram is the sixth most visited website
- Over one billion people use Instagram every month
- Instagram reaches 140 million U.S. users
- 200 million Instagram users visit at least one business profile daily
- 500 million people use Instagram Stories every day
- Twitter has 330 million monthly active users
- YouTube is the second-most popular search engine, behind Google

When you connect with your existing and past clients – your ***sphere of influence*** – on social media platforms like Facebook, Instagram and Twitter, their 338 friends can see your law firm as soon as they "like" and follow your page. This type of online interaction is the most effective way to **monetize your use of digital mediums!**

It's as if your current and past clients sent an email or a text message to all their friends saying, "I recently hired this law firm in our area and I was happy with them. The next time you need this kind of attorney and law firm, I highly recommend them." Gaining exposure to their sphere of influence is powerful.

Another major advantage? They've given you permission to remain top-of-mind with them. As I mentioned, the average user checks in 14 times per day. They log in to read their friends' updates on their Facebook, along with the updates of all the companies and people they have liked, followed, or friended. If you're posting updates to your social media profiles, the people who have followed your page will see that new content whenever they log in.

They will get a notification and see your law firm name. They'll notice a new post, which will pique their interest. Next time they need an attorney in your practice areas, who do you think they'll call?

TOP-OF-MIND AWARENESS (TOMA)

There's a higher probability people who have liked your page will use you again and refer you to their friends because they remember you and their positive experience with your legal representation. They know who you are.

You've remained top-of-mind. Major companies like Coca-Cola, Pepsi, and Lay's spend billions of dollars a year on advertising and promotions, through TV, radio, print, and social media.

What's the whole thought process behind that? They're developing their brand, so they can maintain what the digital marketing industry calls "TOMA," top-of-mind awareness. Leveraging social media inside your existing sphere of influence is an excellent way to tap into that top-of-mind awareness.

With multiple social media platforms and tools, where should you start? What should you be using? In chapter two, we talked about the necessity of publishing blogs to your website on a consistent basis. Today, blogging is an integral component of any social media strategy. Educating your clients is part of a nurturing and trust-building marketing approach. Below are the social media profiles you must set up for your law firm.

FINDING YOUR FOLLOWERS AND CREATING MOMENTUM ONLINE FOR YOUR FIRM

Let's talk strategy before we get into the granular details. How do you leverage social media and gain that initial following?

First, utilize email to stimulate the initial engagement. An active social media profile with daily updates is not worth much if your firm doesn't get "likes" or views.

On the other hand, if thousands of irrelevant people have pressed "like" on your website or on your Facebook Business Page, it won't work to your advantage if they will never need your services. They're not the target market that we discussed in the marketing fundamentals.

Develop a strategy to entice your real clients and the geographic areas you serve to engage with you in social media. As I noted, email marketing is an effective way to direct your clients to your social media profiles. Leveraging email for this purpose is a multiple-step process.

First, build your email list or log into your client relationship management system (if you have one), and export the name and email addresses of your clients. Include current clients, past clients, the sphere of influence of your friends, your business partners, and the people you do business with, and put them into an email.

Queue up a nice message like, "Hey, we appreciate your business. We're becoming active on social media and would love for you to engage with us. Please go to Facebook.com and press the Like button." Don't forget to give them a direct link to your Facebook page.

You can offer them an incentive, something of value like a gift card for a coffee. Or, if you've got an active client base that knows who you are and likes you, just ask them to do it as a favor.

You'll start building your following. But don't stop there because it is not enough to send one email announcing your presence on social media. You want to grow your social media presence as part of your business.

JUST ASK!

In the Google Maps Optimization chapter, I talked about sending an email after the case settles, thanking the client for their business, and asking them to write a review for you on one of the various online directory sites.

Well, there's no reason you couldn't send a subsequent email to that contact a day or two later, which says, "By the way, we're actively involved in social media and would love it if you would engage with us." Then give them a direct link to your social media profiles where they can press like, subscribe, and follow to start engaging with you there.

The key? It must be an automated process where you're typing your client's name and email address. These emails go out to everybody you serve without any hiccups. If you don't send out emails consistently, you won't develop a true following, nor will your real clients engage with you on your social media platforms.

To sum up step one: leverage email to build the initial engagement and following of your real clients. Remember, you want authentic clients, not just throwaway links and subscribers.

Once you've completed the first step, think about what you are going to post. What information are you going to publish? How frequently? You should post to your social media profiles once a day. If that seems like too much for your law firm, post a few times a week at a minimum.

WHAT TO POST (AND WHY)

Your posts should be informative - not a sales pitch. More than 80 percent of the time the content should be social: "Here's a picture of our newest paralegal", "This is what's going on in our practice area", "Here's a picture of our firm at a community event," etc.

Keep it informational, relevant, and social. Beyond that, you must engage. Social media isn't a one-way dialogue. Post updates on your social media profiles that offer engagement opportunities, rather than randomly posting things. Your goal is to inspire people to reply to your posts with reactions like, "Hey, that was funny", or "That's a beautiful picture", or "Thanks for that great tip," all of which enables you to respond.

Then, listen to what your followers are saying. Once you've got a flow – 50, 70, 100 or a couple of thousand people that have liked you – you can hear what they are saying, too. They might post something totally irrelevant to you, like, "Hey, tomorrow's Billy's birthday." In that case, your law firm could reach out and say, "Hey, wish Billy a happy birthday for us!" They will think, "Wow, this is a law firm that cares. They are real and authentic."

Engaging in social media is probably a lost art. Most people that use social media post one-way messages, which completely misses the point. It's a social platform; therefore, there should be a conversation.

FILL IN THE BUSINESS BIO

Next, develop your brand and enhance the bio section on each one of your profiles. Within Facebook, Twitter, and LinkedIn, you will have the option to fill in an 'About Us' or bio section. Publish some interesting information about your law firm there.

Add the information from the 'About Us' page on your website where you talk about where you were founded, why you started the firm, your practice areas, etc., to the bio section on your social media profiles.

You can also put a profile image on each one of these social profiles. Choose an image that represents your law firm. It can either be a headshot of the founder or a logo.

If your personality represents your brand, it is a good idea to use a professional headshot so that people connect and resonate with you. Consumers tend to buy from individuals more than businesses because a business is an anonymous entity, whereas a person is someone that they feel they can get to know, like, and trust.

Be professional. Represent yourself as an important part of the law firm. Stick with the examples on the left – the logo and/or the professional headshot.

It's all about branding. Leverage the header graphic and the image icon. If there is an option to customize the background, do it! Your goal is to align your elements with the overall branding of your law firm.

Everything on your social media profiles must be consistent with your website. Your website features a color scheme, a logo, and a font. Maintain a consistent flow, look, feel, color scheme, and font on all your social media profiles, website, and offline materials.

POSTING PLANS AND POINTERS

Don't forget to have a plan for social media. How often are you going to post? What types of posts are you going to publish? Who is responsible for posting them? How will you engage your clients? Which social media platforms will your law firm use?

Recall that in chapter two we talked about the fundamentals of your marketing plan (market, message, and media). Develop a clear understanding of your ideal client, then craft a message that will resonate with them. All of these are vital factors to consider as part of your social media strategy.

Don't just dive in: take the time to implement a well-thought-out strategy for your posts. Don't make the common mistake of setting up your social profile and publishing posts haphazardly. Instead, consider the following:

- What pages are you going to be on?
- What message are you going to put out?
- What color scheme are you going to use?

After you set that up, home in on your target. Is your ideal client a Baby Boomer who needs an estate plan? Or is it someone who was injured in a car accident and needs a personal injury attorney?

Next, schedule your post types on specific days. For example:

- **Monday** - post a motivational quote to help your clients start their week
- **Tuesday** - feature a team member with a photo and brief bio and/or quote
- **Thursday** - post a client testimonial about your legal services
- **Friday** - post current news pertaining to one of your practice areas. For example, if you're a personal injury attorney, share information about your state's new texting and driving law.

Keep in mind, this is simply an example of an editorial calendar. My point is to make posting to your social media pages as easy as possible by taking the time to plan your posts first. With a streamlined and automated posting process, you can leverage social media without taking up too much of your time.

Leveraging Posts

In the SEO chapter, we discussed the importance of leveraging content. Because content is vital, you must create and post updated information regularly. You can publish your content in various places and automate the posting process to your Facebook and Twitter pages. If the content includes a photo, you can publish it to Pinterest. Syndicate your blog content to recreate compelling social media content.

Remember, content isn't necessarily just written text. You are an expert in your craft. You know things that the average client doesn't, such as what to do in the aftermath of a car accident, or why somebody would choose you instead of another attorney.

You can either write about it, record yourself talking about it, or if you're comfortable on video, use your smartphone to shoot a video talking about an issue your ideal client may be facing.

How 1 Equals 5 - Using videos to optimize your client engagement

Once you make a video, you can get a lot more bang for your buck digitally because that one piece of content can serve multiple functions. The first function can be posting interesting clips and videos on social media or on websites like YouTube or Vimeo.

You can also transcribe the video using a service like castingwords.com. Research the various transcription services available.

The video of you talking about the benefits of your legal experience and customer service can now be transcribed into text, which may then be used as a blog post and be syndicated into your social media profiles. Another step beyond that is to turn that same audio into an audio podcast you host on your website.

There are many options available to repurpose your content working with the modalities that most appeal to you. Some people like to write. Some people like to talk. Some people like to be on video. Figure out what you are most comfortable with and run with that. This is how you create social media content for your online marketing plan.

Remember, educational content that's published in multiple places creates a sense that your firm is accessible and reputable. By publishing and getting picked up in industry listings, the local newspaper, or a reputable blog, you are considered an expert. This is going to increase your credibility, which in turn, will result in more referrals.

Here are some examples of good social media posts:

The following example is a great tip for English spelling. It's, "Here's a look at 11 weird, random facts about English spelling. We're not sure this will make our jobs as expert authors any easier, but it's a nice distraction.

Then, of course, a shortened link back to the website. The point is to give a quick tip like that once a day, keeping you top-of-mind, and helping you to put out fresh, relevant content.

The example below illustrates what you can post on a holiday like Martin Luther King, Jr. Day.

Today we honor the legacy of Dr. Martin Luther King Jr. - a life lived with purpose, integrity and an inspiring commitment to create freedom and equality for all.

What is your favorite Martin Luther King Jr. quote?

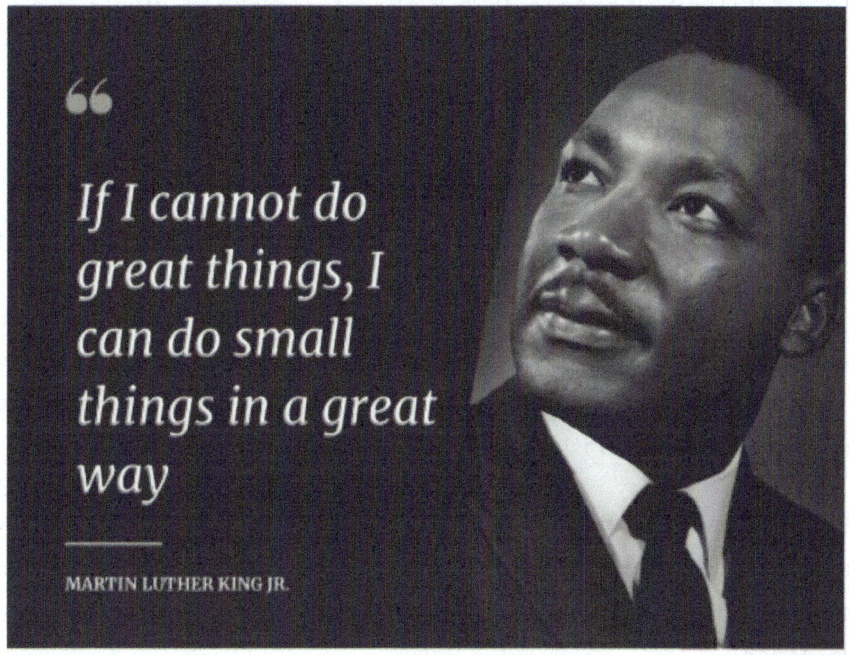

GREATHOUSE

For such an occasion it's easy to find a compelling picture and post it with your own comments to initiate significant engagement from your social media followers. Law firms can also use humor and inspiration/motivation to engage and interact with clients. It's a wonderful way to establish a rapport and lighten up the conversation around legal matters.

Don't forget to acknowledge the various holidays throughout the year with a nice post.

DO'S AND DON'TS OF POSTING:

1. Use the 80/20 rule for marketing messages. Put out 80 percent information and 20 percent marketing.
2. ALWAYS Keep posts business-related. Your political and religious beliefs are never a good mix with business.
3. Photos of your kids playing tee-ball are good, but don't let it dominate your page.
4. Keep your vacation photos on your personal social sites.
5. Keep your business opinions, beliefs, and interests to yourself.

Sometimes knowing what *not* to post is more important than knowing what to post, because the natural tendency is to go to these social media profiles, and just post promotional material.

Law firms make the mistake of assuming they have to appear serious and hard-lined. Creating a message that your firm is made up of people who understand the problems their clients face is a good way to develop a connection!

When and How to Engage

Thus far, we have discussed the importance of asking your clients to 'like you' on Facebook and to write testimonials. We explained why it's vital to interact and respond to your clients' follows and comments with a simple, "Thanks so much for the follow. We appreciate it," and to share their testimonials on your social media platforms. From there, you can also publish these testimonials on your website or embed them on your website with the help of the various widgets and short codes Facebook provides.

Here's another example of a post that creates engagement: "Seniors should live at a place where they are well cared for and respected. If you suspect your loved one is a victim of nursing home negligence, let us know if we can help."

One of your followers reads this and replies, "Wonderful caring staff, lovingly devoted to those they serve." You could then respond, "Thank you for your comment! Our office phone number is 254-1799. We look forward to answering any questions you may have!" Publish posts that make it easy for you to reply to their comments.

Another benefit? Creating engaging posts that provide a way for clients or potential clients to interact offers you an opportunity to gather feedback about what clients and potential clients of law firms in your geographic area are thinking. It's an excellent way to generate repeat or referral business.

If I haven't stressed it enough, I'll say it again. You must have an active presence on social media platforms like Facebook, Instagram, LinkedIn, Twitter, and YouTube. Utilize email marketing to gain an initial following, then post informative, non-sales-oriented updates on a consistent basis and engage.

If you do this regularly and correctly, you'll develop a nice following of real clients in your true service area. You'll remain top-of-mind, which will help you grow your law firm and increase the number of cases you receive via repeat and referral business - the lifeblood of your organization.

Example of a Customized Facebook Page

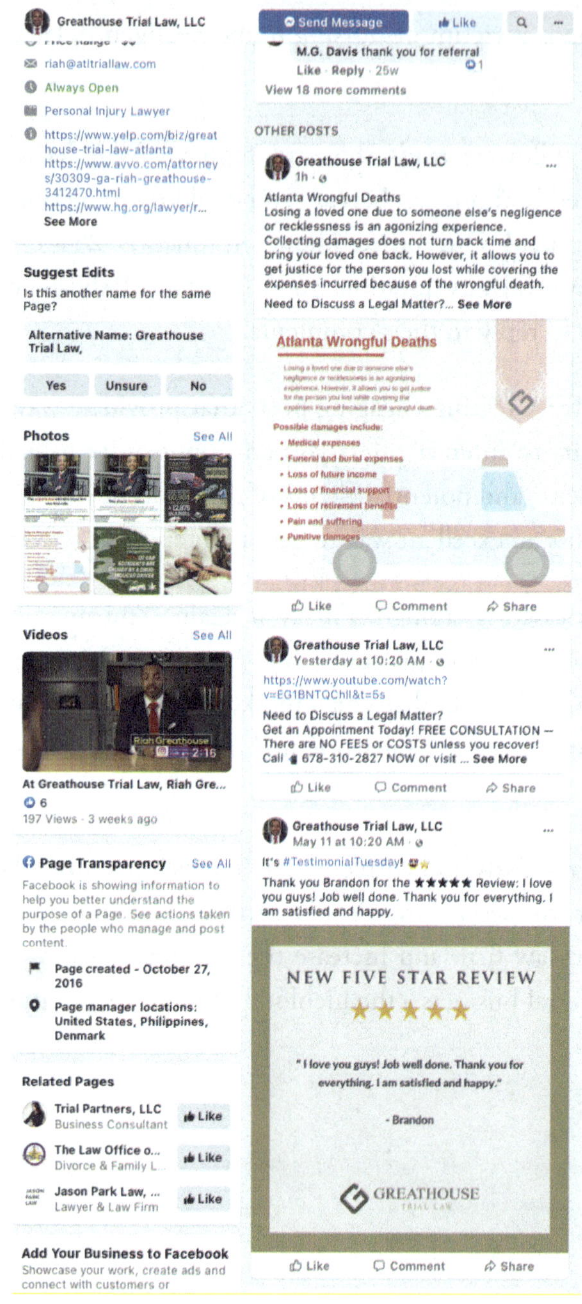

https://www.facebook.com/greathousetriallaw

Example of Branded Twitter Profile:

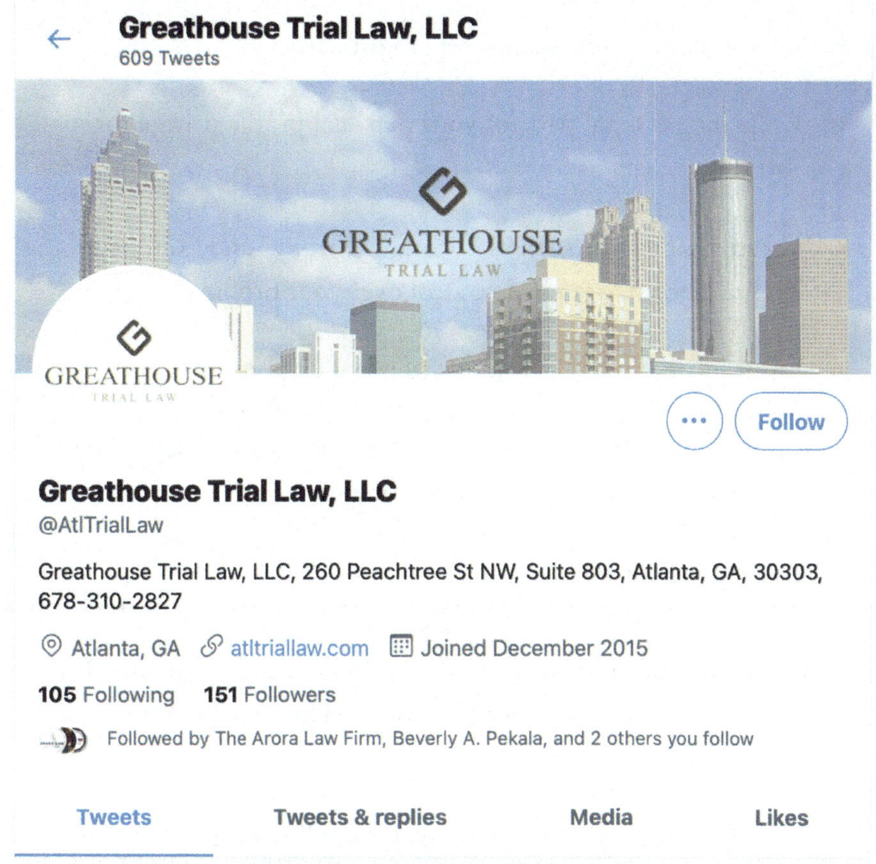

https://twitter.com/AtlTrialLaw

How to Use Facebook for Business

Managing the social media platforms using due diligence can change the fate of your business. Facebook requires users to set up a personal account before they can open a business account. To get started:

PERSONAL FACEBOOK PROFILE

- Fill out your profile completely to earn trust.
- Keep any personal parts of your personal profile private through Settings.
- Create friends lists such as "Work," "Family" and "Limited Profile" for finer-grained control over your profile privacy.
- Limit business contacts' access to personal photos.
- Post a professional or business casual photo of yourself on your personal profile to reinforce your brand.

BUSINESS FACEBOOK PAGE

- Establish a business account if you don't already have one. It is similar to creating a personal account. The page looks like the following:
- Be sure to read the Facebook rules regarding business accounts.
- Combine Facebook with other social media tools like Twitter. For example, when someone asks a question on Twitter, you can respond in detail in a blog post and link to it from Facebook. However, be careful before integrating your Twitter feed into your Facebook profile, as a stream of tweets can seem overwhelming to your contacts.
- Post your newsletter subscription information and archives somewhere in your profile.
- Obtain a Facebook vanity URL so that people can find you easily.

- Add your Facebook URL to your email signature and any marketing collateral (business cards, etc.) so prospects can learn more about you.

- Post business updates on your professional page. Focus on business activities, such as "Working with system technologies on website redesign."

- Share useful articles and links and valuable resources that interest clients and prospects to establish credibility.

- Add social networking buttons to your website.

- Suggest Friends to clients and colleagues. By helping them, you establish trust.

- Buy Facebook ads to target your exact audience.

- Join network, industry, and alumni groups related to your law firm.

One of the biggest benefits social networking platforms like Facebook provide the business community? The ability to get repeat exposure with the people in your network leads to word-of-mouth referrals, too. Clients, peers, and prospects can comprise your network. And you can promote events and other law-firm-related news through your Facebook profile. These are common and essential tactics to implement on Facebook for your business.

How to Avoid Mistakes on Facebook

With 2.8 billion monthly active users as of the last quarter of 2020, Facebook has become a must-use marketing platform for businesses of all sizes. While Facebook's staggering membership stats alone are enough to entice small business owners, few actually know how to do so effectively.

Here are 10 of the most common Facebook marketing mistakes business owners make and how you can avoid them.

1. **Not having a clear marketing purpose:** Whether you've created a page for Facebook or are still working on it, now is a good time to evaluate what you want to get out of it. So set clear goals at the very beginning.

   For example, suppose you are hoping to attract 500 new followers who could become potential clients in a six-month time period. Be sure to assign someone within your company to maintain the page. It's important to regularly post fresh content on the page. If you've already created your page but it hasn't been updated in a while, update it as soon as possible.

2. **Not knowing the difference between a personal profile and a business page:** There are so many major differences between personal and business pages on Facebook. You should know what they are so that you stay safely within Facebook's Terms of Service.

   A personal profile is the type of account an individual shares with friends and family. But a Facebook business page is used by brands and companies for promotional purposes.

   Another important distinction: If you have a Facebook page for your business, you have followers and likes. If you have a personal profile, you've got friends. So, don't ask your potential clients to become your "friend" on Facebook. They must follow and like your business page.

3. **Not understanding how your clients use Facebook:** Many small business owners don't know how their clients interact with Facebook. When you log into your Facebook account, for instance, the first thing you see is your newsfeed and the posts from business pages you have liked and followed. It's important to understand that marketing your business page is not the same as posting a status update to your friends through your personal Facebook account. If you want to get your

followers to view your content, post directly on the Facebook page for your business. Your posts will show up on newsfeeds.

4. **Not getting the right URL for your Facebook page:** You also need to know how to obtain the proper URL for your business page on Facebook. There are so many business owners who don't understand that if you have 25 likes/followers on your business page, you are eligible to obtain a URL for your page with your law firm's name in it.

   For example, it could be www.facebook.com/yourlawfirmname instead of the former random number URL assigned. You can go directly to www.facebook.com/username and log in to choose your URL.

5. **Not responding to comments:** Remember, Facebook is all about interaction. It's very important you quickly respond to potential clients if they post questions on your business page.

   The faster you can answer their question, the higher the likelihood of converting that potential client into an actual client. You can adjust your Facebook page settings to notify you via email whenever someone posts a new comment on your business page.

6. **Creating fake Facebook user accounts to boost follower count:** It is a long-term process to get potential clients and existing ones to become followers of your business Facebook page. Although you may want to see your follower count increase rapidly, don't give in to the temptation to create fake Facebook accounts and then become a follower of your business page using that particular account. Facebook can often detect fake accounts, which are a violation of their Terms of Service. If you're caught, you will lose your page and the marketing power that comes with it.

7. **Not updating the page regularly:** You should not create a page for your business and let it become inactive. You should update it with fresh content at least two times a week. This will help keep your followers engaged and interested in your brand.

8. **Post purposeful, quality content:** Every post should have a purpose. Some examples of purposeful posts include: demonstrating your experience in an area of law, inspiring your audience with a motivational quote, engaging them to answer a question or participate in your post, educating them through an infographic about your area of law, sharing client reviews, and promoting your firm.

   Nothing irritates a potential client like poor content. Consumers are always looking for useful information, not hype. Before you post anything, ask yourself how your content benefits your followers. If you can't answer that question, revise before you post it.

9. **Not using Facebook's free tools:** One of the great things about Facebook is that it offers several free tools to help businesses gauge how well they are using their page to attract and engage clients. There are many free tools in Facebook that provide business owners with detailed metrics about the effectiveness of their page content, analysis of user growth and demographics, and other concerns. You can find out more about it by logging on to https://developers.facebook.com/docs/platforminsights/page.

10. **Not properly promoting your page:** Many business owners aren't aware of the ways in which they can promote their Facebook page and attract potential clients. Facebook offers an advertising option that allows you to purchase relatively inexpensive ads. You can pay to boost your post. For example, if you've written a post about the best strategies for designing a good website, you can promote that post on Facebook through its advertising and sponsorship platform. You can also create a link to your Facebook page on your company website.

HOW TO SET UP A FACEBOOK BUSINESS PROFILE

As one of the top social networking websites, Facebook provides you an opportunity to create a business profile. It is another method for your company to reach its marketing goals.

With a business page, you can create advertisements that appear on targeted Facebook pages and allow you to reach a wider audience. So now with just an email address, you can quickly set up and customize your own business account on Facebook.

Here are a few steps detailing how to create your business profile in Facebook:

1. Access the Facebook website and click the "Create a Page for a celebrity, band or business" link at the bottom of the "Sign Up" section.

2. Choose the "Business or Brand" option.

3. Type in the page name you want to use and select your business category.

4. Add pictures.

5. Create a username for your page. (e.g. the name your clients will use to search for you)

6. Add your business details, such as the "about" section.

7. Add additional keywords that people might use to search for your service offerings.

8. Fill in all details; contact information, location, hours of operation and other information you want visitors to know.

9. Tell your story – e.g. what sets you apart from your competitors, how you got started, how long you've been in business, etc.

Create content for your page, before asking your clients to "like" your page.

HOW TO CREATE YOUR FOLLOWING IN FACEBOOK

Once the business page is complete, most people are anxious to get lots of followers. The truth is it takes time to build a new follower base from scratch.

Efforts to build your base should begin the day you set up a Facebook page. Creating a strong following requires an ongoing commitment to the brand, and monitoring and networking with people who find interest in your area of law. Besides quality service, it's important to build close-knit relationships with clients and potential clients.

If successfully applied, the tips below can increase your following:

1. Be Prepared with Quality Posts and Consistent Engagement

If you want to be liked, be likable first. A disorganized Facebook page can turn off clients instantly. When reviewing a Facebook page, quality content and active engagements make excellent first impressions.

Several other factors people look for before joining a page include the brand itself, consistent posting of fresh information, and active engagement from both followers and administrators.

2. Reward Your Loyal Supporters

You may have just started your Facebook page, but your business is well-established. Encourage your loyal clients to join your Facebook page as supporters and reward them with customizable badges/tabs (to be placed on their profiles for visibility) for consistent support. A review from a happy client is much more attractive than a marketing slogan, creating irresistible appeal for that 'Like' button.

3. Leverage Your Existing Social Networks

If you've built a strong Instagram network for your business, utilize it to promote your Facebook page. Some people prefer not to overlap similar social contacts on both accounts, but why diminish your chance to be noticed? Your followers can broadcast your message on both of their social platforms by reaching out to a greater audience about your business.

4. Integrate Social Buttons to Your Website

It's essential to have a main hub correlating all your social media activities. Your company's website is the only place that gives you full control over content and brand management. Integrate social media buttons to encourage connections.

5. Take the Initiative: Request Help from Friends

It's difficult to start a business page with no engagement whatsoever. Why not initiate messages to your friends and family who support your law firm?

Ask them to help in some discussions, reward them with publicity or return the favor. It's easier to ask a friend than a stranger if you're worried about spamming people.

Make sure the question is interesting enough to initiate a conversation. If you use your personal account and business page strategically, you'll discover a huge advantage of getting new friends to be your followers while they're getting to know you better.

6. Participate Outside Your Page

Use the Facebook Directory and Facebook Search to locate other Facebook pages in your niche and look for public discussions based on search terms related to your business.

Provide value to the popular pages; build credibility and relationships with the administrators and members. Get to know them better before asking them to look at your page. They just may reward you publicly.

7. Collaborate with Other Page Administrators for a Social Event

You can collaborate with other page admins to create a special event that may benefit both your followers and bring in new connections. For example, take a video and photos of a charity event you're involved in, post them on your business page, and tag the people you worked with. It will create a sense of community, and because people want to support their communities, they'll remember you for your involvement. The next time they need an attorney in your area of law, guess who they will contact?

HOW TO BUILD YOUR BRAND AND MARKET ON FACEBOOK

A large portion of web users today are spending their time and attention on Facebook, and this includes business owners. However, most marketers lack comprehensive knowledge about how to implement Facebook for marketing their brand.

It is true that like any other social media platform, Facebook also demands some strategies to be performed to brand your business page.

Facebook offers many tools and apps to build a strong brand. Here are three chief tools to know and understand:

Tools for Guerilla Marketers

For the guerilla marketers who are very aggressive, Facebook offers a bevy of viral channels to get the word out to your friends and creatively reach your target audience.

There are so many aspects of guerilla marketing tactics, but the best part is that it is totally free. Everyone on Facebook can use these strategies to recruit and evangelize their causes. Some of the best guerilla tools are:

- **Profile Page:** Your profile page is the starting point on Facebook. It is basically the landing page that you design in order to convert your friends to engage with certain parts of your identity.

  Your profile page is an opportunity to craft a credible real-world story around the reasons your services are valuable. Take advantage of Personal Info, Work Info, Photos, and applications to tell bits and pieces of your narrative as it relates to your brand.

- **Facebook Groups:** Groups are the oldest and simplest way to build a community around your brand or company on Facebook. By starting a group, you create a central place for clients, partners, and friends to participate in conversations around your brand. Here you can post discussion topics, photos, videos, and links right out of the box.

- **Facebook Events:** Facebook Events is a free application developed by Facebook that anyone can use to promote marketing events, sponsored parties, or even product launches, transactions, or company milestones.

- **Facebook and Instagram Messenger:** Facebook and Instagram private messages (PMs) can be a powerful vehicle for targeted marketing. Messages are like email, except a lot less fully-featured – Facebook and Instagram allow you to search, sort, filter, categorize, or star messages.

Facebook Tools for Advertisers

Depending on your budget, you can get started as an advertiser on Facebook with as little as a few dollars by promoting your business page through paid ads. Some Tools Related to this Field are:

- **Ads:** Facebook offers advertisers several different types of ads. The type you choose will depend on the goal you have for the ad.
    - Brand awareness image ads
    - Local awareness ads
    - Video ads
    - Link click ads

- **Polls:** Polls offer an easy way for marketers to quickly conduct research within their targeted audience.

- **Facebook Notifications:** Notifications have been proven to be an effective tool for retaining existing users of your app. However, notifications get less press than feed items and invitations because they're not as effective at spreading your app.

HOW TO CONVERT YOUR FACEBOOK TRAFFIC INTO SALES

There is no doubt that today Facebook has become the leader in social media platforms. It is also useful for business owners and Internet marketers who use it to take advantage of this social media platform to promote their business.

Facebook helps them to create their own business page, build their brand name and also get traffic. Millions of people are today using Facebook, so it is a great marketing tool for you.

However, converting your business page traffic into potential sales takes time. There are various ways to use your Facebook Business Page to generate more traffic into sales for your business.

Here are 10 effective tips to use Facebook business Page effectively to get sales:

1. **Offer Ultimate Communication with Your Audience**

   Facebook people are very active; they will always check their Facebook accounts often just to update their status. After creating your business page if you don't provide the same active communication with your audience, then you'll lose their attention very quickly.

   You need to update your page often just to remind your audience that you are there and active. You should also answer the questions promptly if your audience asks something. This builds trust between your business and your potential clients. The more you can earn credibility with your clients the more you will get sales.

2. **Advertise Your Business Page with Facebook Ads**

   If you already built your business page you can create buzz regarding your business on Facebook. You can get your page noticed by investing a small amount of money to promote your business page. Without properly promoting your business page you likely won't get noticed.

   When you promote your page using Facebook Ads, it won't sound like you're pitching Facebook users with a blatant sales page. If you use your business page as your landing page in your Facebook Ads, then more new readers will come to your business page because they perceive your ad not as a sales page, but as an interesting page that they want to explore. Automatically your traffic will convert into sales.

3. **Provide Useful Information, Not Just Product Promotion**

   You should also balance your business page with useful information related to your niche. Using your business page as your prime promotional tool to promote your product will be less effective because most Facebook users aren't ready to buy anything yet.

   They came to Facebook for fun, social interaction, and information exchange. They'll love your business page if you provide them with good information. Instead of solely promotional posts, use your business page to educate your clients. When they find interest in your information, that will lead to an interest in your business which will lead to sales.

4. **Show Your Visitors You Are Different**

   Show your Facebook visitors how you're different and why they should use your legal services instead of your competitors.

   Suppose you provide legal services in the personal injury area of law. You might say something like: "We distinguish ourselves from other personal injury firms by noting that there are no fees until we win your case."

5. **Promote on Other Sites**

   You should put your Facebook business page button on your company blog, websites, and other social network sites. The more sites that have your links the more people have an opportunity to sign up on your business page. By getting more visitors you will get more chances to obtain leads and, ultimately, clients.

6. **Maintain Uniqueness**

   Facebook has 2.45 billion users. It's not possible for all business pages to attract all users one at a time. Your goal is to attract your ideal clients. If you want to stand apart from the competition you should maintain a unique business page to your niche.

   Look at related pages in your niche just to see what others are doing. Take notes and think about how you can make your business page better because this will help build brand recognition.

These marketing strategies should allow you to generate more sales for your business. Taking time to implement these strategies will provide you with many more opportunities to reach your target client.

CHAPTER TEN

Video Marketing – How You Can Tap into the POWER of YouTube AND other Video Sharing Websites to Enhance Your Visibility and Drive Better Conversion

Did you know that YouTube ranks second in search engines? Yes, it's even ahead of Bing & Yahoo!

Oftentimes, when law firms are extremely focused on search engine optimization, they neglect the opportunities provided by video and YouTube. Implementing a video marketing strategy for your law firm can get you additional placement in the search results for your targeted keywords both organically and via PPC (YouTube ads), enhance the effectiveness of your SEO efforts, and improve visitor conversion.

WHY USE VIDEO MARKETING?

There are a number of reasons to use video marketing for your law firm.

First, it will increase your exposure on the search engines, giving you more placeholders for your most important keywords. Video marketing will enhance your SEO effort by driving visitors to your website and creating relevant links to your website, which will improve conversions. It can also add to your overall credibility and ubiquity since video is another place people can discover and learn about what you do, how you do it and what makes your firm different (and better) than competing firms.

Once a potential client lands on your website, if you've posted a compelling video on the homepage and on the subpages, it will resonate deeper with them than a website devoid of video. Video helps convert your visitors from casual browsers of your website to potential clients that pick up the phone and call your office.

Embedding the appropriate video(s) onto your website and also PPC landing pages provides visitors who prefer video over reading another form of engagement that can enhance conversion.

Currently (although this is rapidly changing), there are fewer videos than there are web pages on the Internet. Thus, creating relevant, high-quality video content for YouTube and other video-sharing sites is a somewhat underutilized yet effective method for persuading clients to contact you. Such videos will help you connect with people and answer their questions when they're seeking information on the area of law that you practice.

I mentioned that you can show up in search engines with an image next to your video, and obtain multiple placeholders on Google for your most important keywords. Here is a screenshot to illustrate my point, using the example of "Divorcing A Narcissist." You can see that my client, Florida

Women's Law Group, is three of the top five law firms on this search results page:

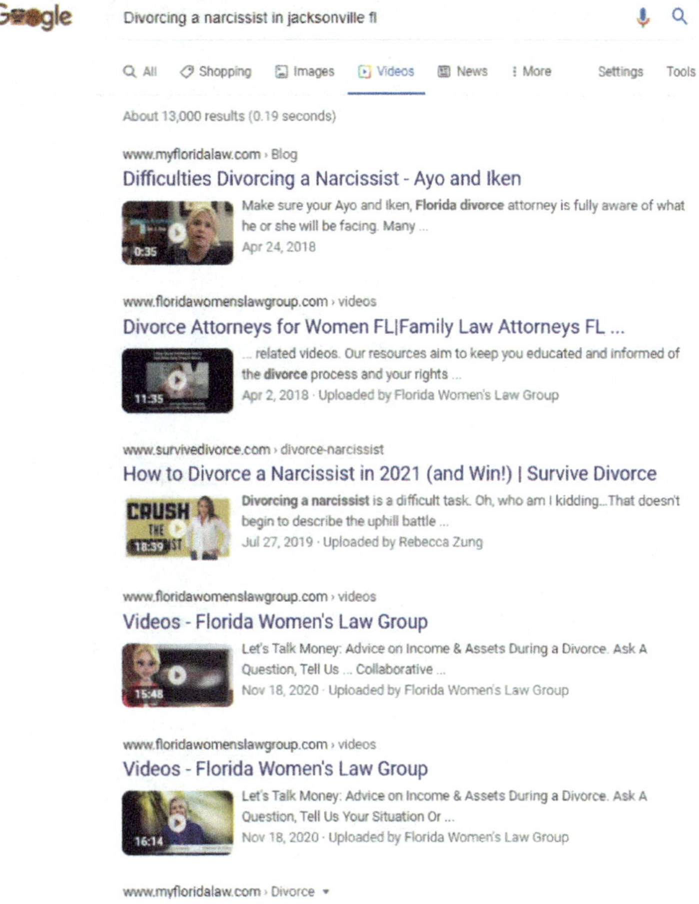

This family law firm prefers to focus on narcissistic divorces and custody battles because they're more contentious, which typically means more billable hours in order to get the client their desired result. Florida Women's Law Group's videos have been optimized, along with their website, for various permutations of narcissist-related keywords, among other semantically related words like "divorcing someone with a personality disorder". If you do this right and optimize your videos correctly (I'm going to explain how to do it in this chapter), your video will show up in the natural search results on the Google videos tab, which is extremely powerful but potentially can even appear somewhere within Google's general search results (first few pages typically but varies widely based on the type of search phrase). Doing this gives you the opportunity to have more placeholders for the various services that you provide.

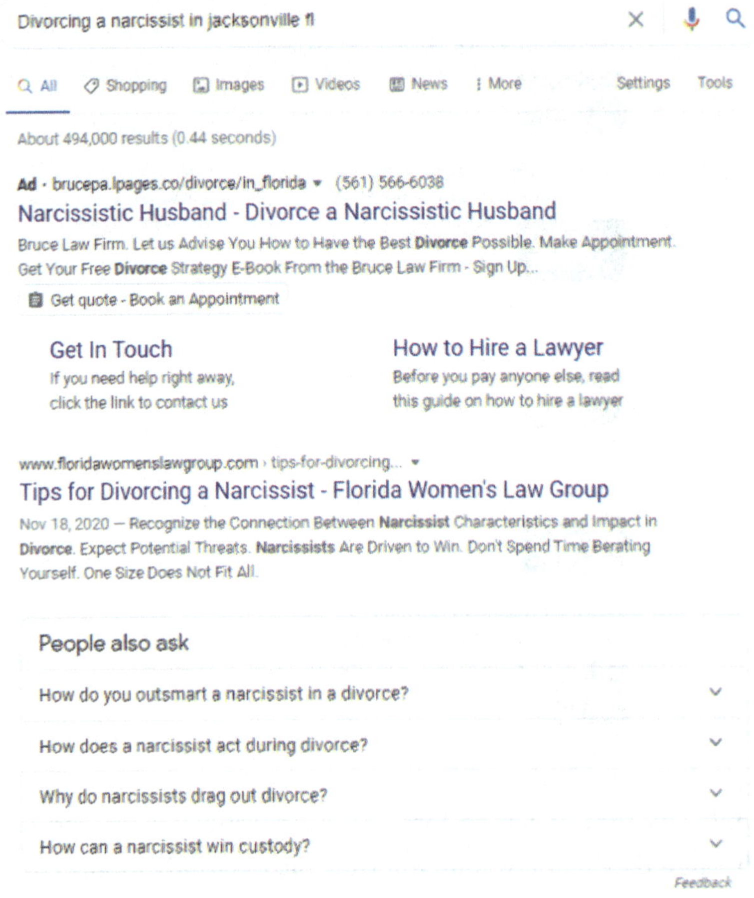

In the case above, this blog post is optimized for "Divorcing a Narcissist." The website and these videos show up in an organic search on a couple of different pages. You can see examples of this through a variety of keywords. Not only will your website show up, but your properly optimized video can show up in that search too.

Whether your video ranks number one, number two, or number three, most of the time you'll notice that the video receives a much higher clickthrough rate. Why? Because it features a large image previewing video. Where are you going to click when you're searching: a static piece of text or the image? Much attention goes to those video results. In this chapter, I'll explain how to incorporate and optimize these types of videos for your services in your market.

VIDEO HELPS WITH YOUR OVERALL SEO EFFORT

Another objective we can accomplish with video is the enhancement of our SEO efforts. As covered in the SEO chapter, links are critical for ranking. By creating good video content, you can drive inbound links to your website from high-level video sites like YouTube and Vimeo.

As a reminder, don't just post the generic Home, About Us, Our Services, Contact Us pages on your website. Publish a page for each of your core services. Videos that link to those pages will help with that SEO effort. Additionally, video content on the pages of your website will reduce your bounce rate and increase the time visitors spend on your site. These are vital SEO factors.

'Bounce rate' refers to somebody getting to your page and clicking back immediately or browsing away. Google understands those actions as the page not being relevant to that search.

If the majority of the people that arrive on your site click off and leave right away, it results in a high bounce rate. Therefore, Google will start to show you less prominently in their results. That's part of the Google algorithm. The other factor is the amount of time spent on the site. If somebody gets to your page, stays there for ten seconds, and moves on, the visit might not be considered a bounce, but Google still looks at the length of time spent on the site.

If you have a video and a visitor takes the time to watch it in its entirety, it improves your website visit length statistics. Even if they only watch a couple of seconds of the video, you have captured their attention long enough that Google will notice that your site is relevant.

Don't get confused by the notion that having video on your page automatically improves your SEO. That's not necessarily the case. However, visitors remaining on your page longer and not bouncing off does impact SEO. Here's an example of how you can drive some links with your videos.

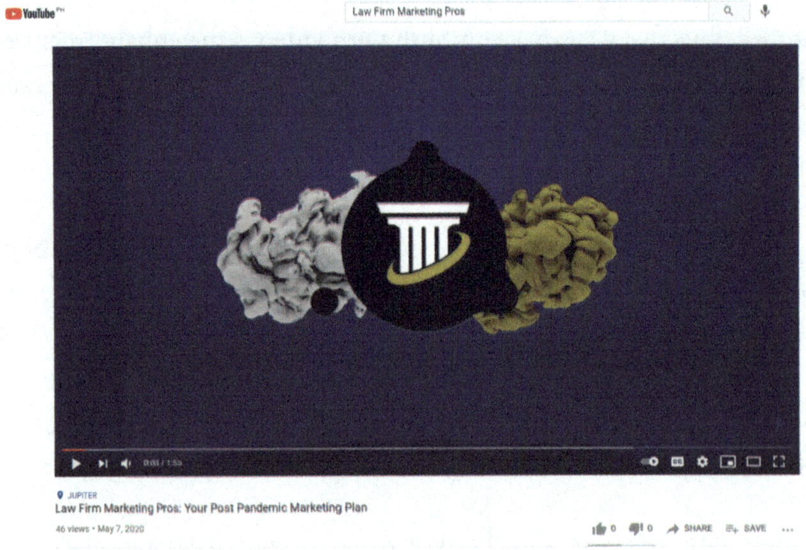

In May of 2020, I released my "Post Pandemic Marketing Plan" video on YouTube as we were phasing out of lockdowns. In the description area, we included our website link: www.LawFirmMarketingPros.com.

This relevant, high-impact link now connects a viewer from YouTube to our site. You can do the same thing. I suggest that you link it either to the homepage, or a subpage specific to that topic if you have one.

If a consumer is interested in your service offering, they will most likely watch the video on the homepage. People like to watch videos. Again, this will help you improve visitor time on your site, decrease the bounce rate, and increase potential conversions. It's rare to find a video on subpages, but if you do publish video content on the homepage banner or on your services page, your visitors will take a couple of minutes to watch. Why? Video is unexpected and more interesting than text alone. People enjoy watching someone explain the topic that they are researching.

Here's another example. I always recommend that your homepage is above the fold.

The Most Important Thing Attorneys Can Do Today For Digital Marketing

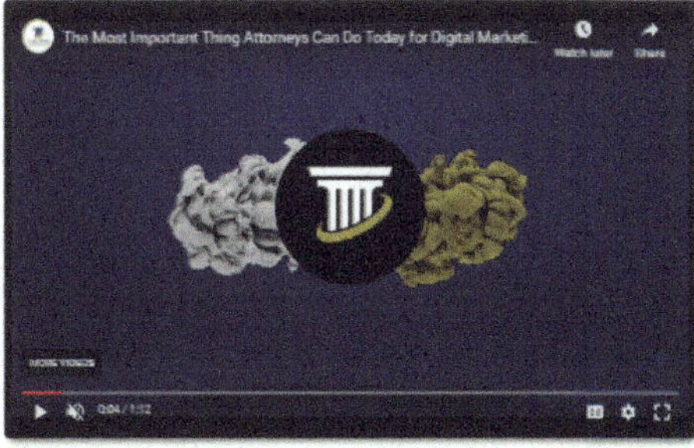

Above the Fold

Keeping a video above the fold means consumers don't have to scroll down to see the most important information. Notice that as soon as this page is pulled up you immediately see the video.

You will want to do the same, providing an intro video about who you are and what you do. That video, placed correctly above the fold, will improve on-page site time and reduce your bounce rate.

I've mentioned the fact that **video gives you more placement in GOOGLE searches.** It's going to give you better search engine optimization because you get the links from the video sites, you're improving your time on site, and reducing your bounce rate.

But the biggest, most powerful benefit of video is that **it will improve conversions**. You can have the best SEO strategy in the world and drive hundreds of qualified people to your home page or your subpages daily. But if they don't call you to schedule a consultation and retain you as their attorney, you're missing a major opportunity. Your website is not converting leads into clients.

Improving Conversions with Video

Publishing intelligent videos on your website will improve your conversions because video clips resonate with consumers. Video gives them the chance to get to know, like, and trust you before they call you, especially if you follow my strategy rather than create a traditional corporate video.

To improve your conversion rate, create an authentic video of your team or you talking directly to the camera. Connect with your audience on an emotional level, answer their questions, and give them a strong call to action, such as "Call now to schedule your free consultation."

Consider making a 30-second video for every Holiday, wishing your visitors "Happy Holidays," "Happy New Year," or a safe Memorial Day Weekend.

Consumers connect in a variety of ways to visual media: readers will read all the content on a page; listeners will choose to listen to audio offerings, if your website contains embedded podcasts or other audio files; and others prefer something visual because motion gets their attention. By providing video on your website, combined with text, you can connect not only with visually-oriented consumers but every type of consumer. You'll ensure that you do not miss an opportunity to engage with people who connect exclusively with video because they would not take the time to read a plain text web page.

Here's a website of an online institute that offers private investigation training.

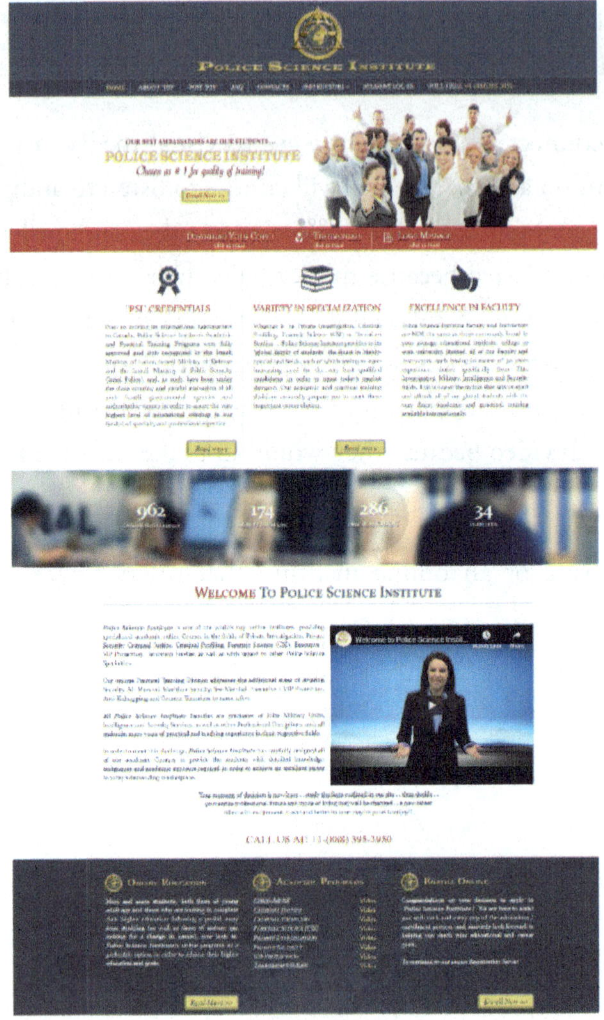

Upon visiting their website, you will see both the text and a video that explains what PSI has to offer. If you watch the video and hear the speaker say something that's relevant to you and makes you feel connected, you might think, "Great! This is definitely the right institute for me." Do you think you would be more apt to call him over somebody who doesn't have that type of messaging on their website?

Adding video to your website will improve your conversion rates and make your phone ring more often.

LEVERAGING VIDEO

Now that we understand the power of video and its ability to:

- Improve Your SEO
- Achieve Better Placement on the Search Engines

Help with Conversion

How can we leverage it? How can we optimize this critical asset?

Create simple videos about your law firm, your services, and your most frequently asked questions. Next, upload these videos to YouTube and other video-sharing sites, and syndicate them to your website and social media profiles.

What type of video should you create? Remember, people resonate with people. Keep it simple and be authentic and personable. Show your face or the face of someone who represents your law firm, to the camera. Be frank and to the point. It doesn't have to be a 20-minute video. In fact, the best length is between **30 seconds to three minutes**, enough to communicate the message that you are accessible and trustworthy. Research shows that most consumers bail after 90 seconds.

Don't Overthink It! You Don't Need a High-End Video to Have an Impact.

Don't feel like you have to go all out and hire a high-end production crew or buy an HD camera to create videos. You can create video clips using the technology you already have. If you've got a smartphone or a webcam, you have the ability to create video content that will work for your website.

You don't need high-end editing software either. YouTube gives you the ability to upload regular video and edit it right within the system. By edit,

I mean cropping and tailoring the video to begin and end where you wish. You can put your phone number down in the bottom area of the video as well as a link to your website. Or you can use simple editing software like iMovie (free with Macintosh computers) and Movie Maker (free with the PC).

Using the technology you have, stand in front of your law firm sign with your logo or in your office, and talk to the camera. Address the people who visit your website because they will remember.

What Kind of Videos Should You Create?

The first video ought to be an introduction for your website in which you introduce your firm to potential clients in an approachable manner to establish immediate rapport.

Your message can be as simple as, "Thank you so much for visiting our law firm (NAME of FIRM'S) website. We specialize in providing XYZ services to the XYZ area. Some of the features that make us unique include: (list a few specific areas of your firm's focus.) We'd love the opportunity to serve you. Give us a call right away at the number below to schedule your free consultation." A simple video along those lines is the necessary first step in your plan.

Your other videos should discuss your primary areas of practice, which ties in well with the SEO strategy we discussed previously. Dedicate a page of your website to each area of law you practice.

If you are a business law attorney, you do not simply provide general business services. You offer business formation, contracts, shareholder agreements/disputes, operating agreements, litigation, intellectual property, trademarks, employment, franchise law, and more. Make a list of the services to which you want to attract more business and shoot a brief video about each.

Phase two involves a powerful piece of content known as frequently asked questions (FAQs). Write down the most common questions people ask, then create a video about them. If we continue with the business law example, you could record videos about what to do if your business gets sued; why you should always have an operating agreement; and why you should protect your intellectual property. Get creative!

While this information is obvious to you, the average consumer does not know what you know. Creating a short video that provides answers to these frequently asked questions makes for great content on your YouTube channel, to be syndicated on your social media profiles, and/or uploaded to your blog on your website.

Sharing Your Message

Now that you know what types of videos you want to create and how to go about it, what should you say? Should you have a script or just wing it? Consumers relate to authentic, natural, and real people. If you must use a script because you're not comfortable without one, do your best to sound unscripted. However, if you can get in front of a camera and speak as you would to a client in your office in person about your services, that will work best.

What to Say

Here is a simple script you can follow:

> "At -------- Law Firm, we provide a full range of legal services (to the specific area, whatever area you're in, or whatever area of law this video is about)."

Include a brief description of what you do in that area, then say, "If you're in need of this service in your area, we can help. Call our office today at 555-5555."

If you are a personal injury attorney focusing on auto accidents, your page might say:

> "Being involved in a car accident is a life-changing experience. From expensive medical bills to being forced to buy a new vehicle, it seems like the ordeal will never end. If you weren't responsible for the accident, the situation is even more upsetting. Not only must you try to rebuild your life, but you must also live with the knowledge that the entire problem could have been avoided which can be absolutely devastating. The last thing you need is the additional stress of being bullied and given the run-around from insurance companies. Our job is to give you peace of mind and be your partner through the process of getting you the compensation that you deserve. Fortunately, you may be able to recover some of your financial losses by filing a claim against the party responsible for the accident."

A simple video for each one of your services should always include a call to action telling them what to do. And if you're a personal injury attorney, let them know there's no fee unless there's a settlement or verdict. They do not pay anything upfront.

Don't overthink this part of the process. Consider your core services, then shoot a quick, 30-second to a one-and-a-half-minute video about each area your firm focuses on. Keep it brief and informative.

What to Do with Your Video Content

What should you do with the videos once you've got them? Set up a YouTube channel. Go to YouTube.com. Upload your video and name it correctly and intelligently, by putting it in terms people will use when searching. If somebody is looking for a family lawyer who focuses on child custody, they will type in "your city family law attorney," or they might go deeper and search for "your city child custody attorney." Name the video using your keywords.

When you upload it to YouTube, title it "Denver Family Law Attorneys" or "Denver Child Custody Attorney," then add a description with a link to your site: "Visit us online at yourlawfirm.com/childcustodyattorneys" and then include a description about what you do, briefly outlining what you said in your video.

YouTube Best Practices - Citation Development is KEY

Here's a good example of a bad example.

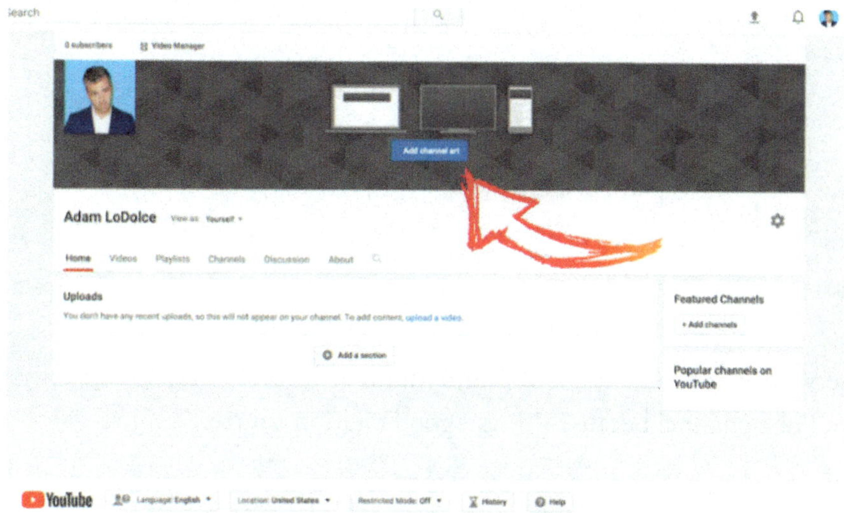

When you set up your channel, give it a "city plus service, name of your law firm" title, instead of just your law firm name. Add tags with keywords to it.

Do NOT leave the tag area blank.

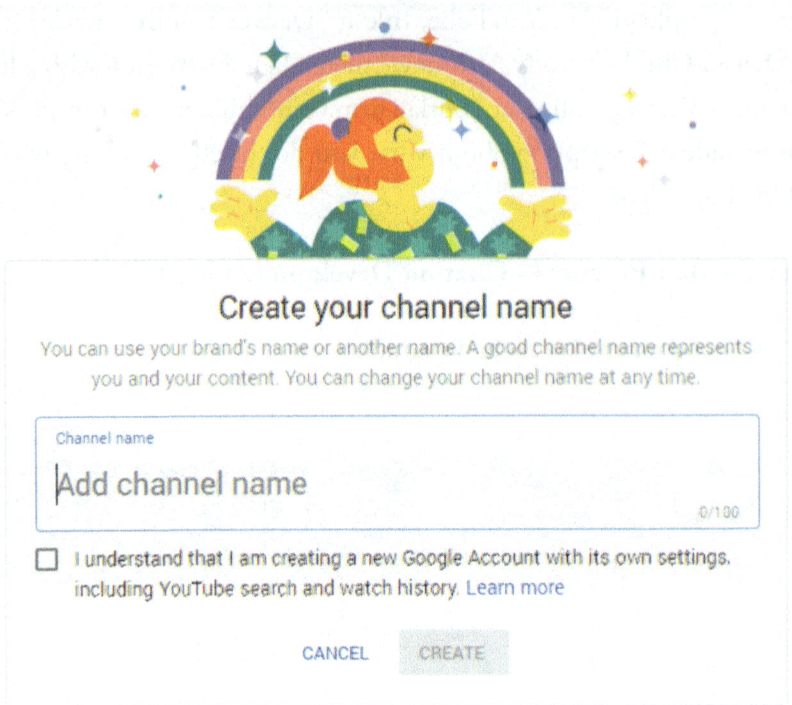

Use your name, address, and phone number in every description on your YouTube channel because this is a good citation source.

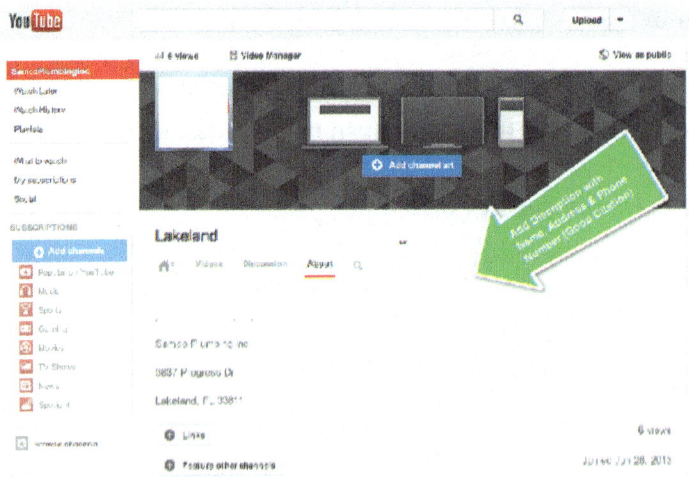

As covered in the Google Maps optimization chapter, citation development is critical (having your law firm name, address, and phone number referenced consistently across the web). This is a great place to obtain citations. Also, upload an image avatar with your law firm logo. You can replace the default image with your logo or a picture of the team or office.

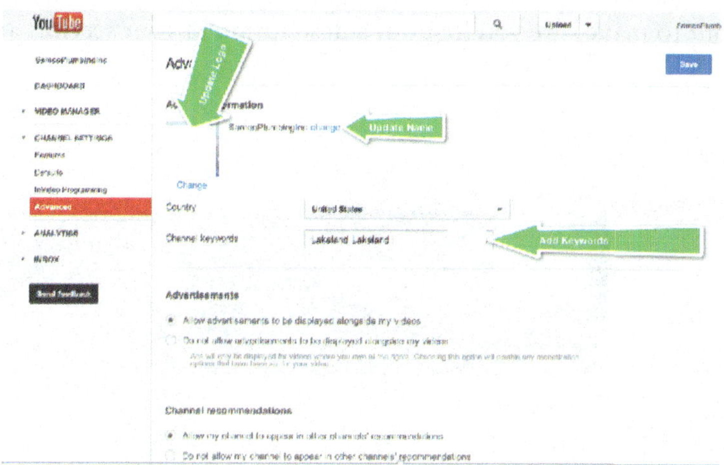

Here's a visual representation. If you log into YouTube and create your channel, you'll get an email confirmation. Once you're set-up, you can go to the "My Channel" settings and make some of the updates I referenced on the previous slide.

To change your logo, simply click "change" and choose your image–a very simple step.

Where it says, "Your company name," it's going to default to something basic such as your email address on Google. You can hit "change" and update it to say, "your city family law lawyer" or "your city child custody law" and then a dash and your law firm name.

This gives you the chance to get your YouTube channel itself to show up for your keywords in the search engine. You will also have the opportunity to add your channel keywords. That is where you can type in words such as "your city criminal defense attorney," "your city DUI lawyer," "your city battery law firm," and of course your law firm name.

From there, there's a section where you can click "About your company" and put a description about who you are, what you do, and what areas you serve. You can get as creative with this area as you want, but it is most important to make sure you first put a description of your services and your city.

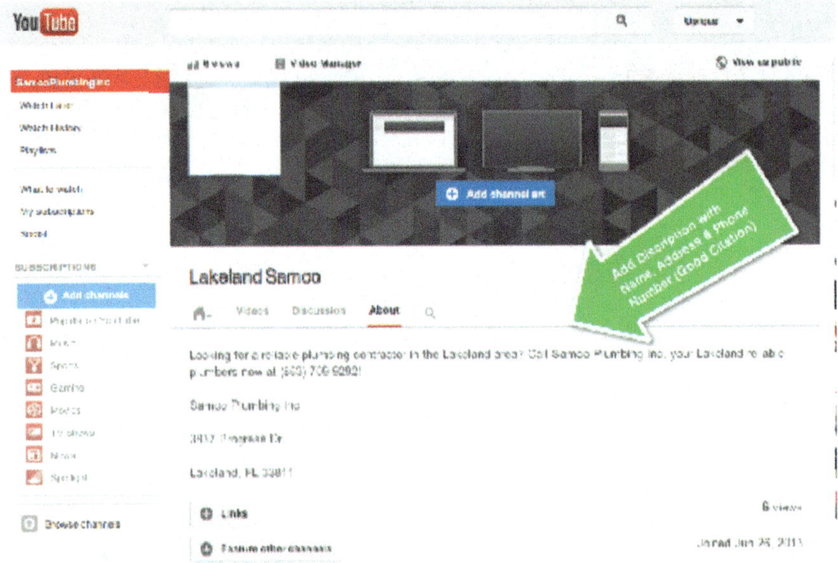

If you're in Tampa, you put Tampa. If you're in Lakeland, you put Lakeland. If you're in Los Angeles, you put Los Angeles. Put your phone number and, again, restate your name, address, and phone number. Citations are important. Having this in the description area is a powerful citation source.

Always put your name, address, and phone number the same way as you did on your Google Map listing, your Lawyers.com, etc. That way, you will be consistent across the web, improving the probability of ranking in the Google Map listings.

Video Tagging Best Practices

Now, let's talk about video tagging best practices. Let's say you created the inventory of videos I recommended: an intro video and clips for each of your services.

How did you tag those videos to maximize the opportunity and to make sure you're going to rank well in search?

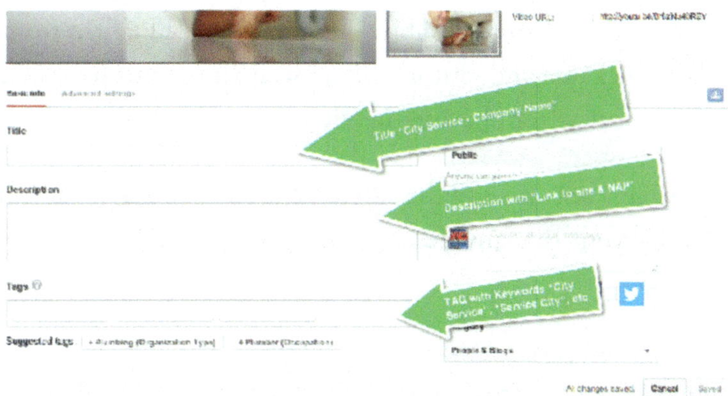

- Title Video with City Service - Law Firm Name (always mix up the services section)

- The description should always start with http://url.com and then describe the service using those same keywords. ALWAYS ADD N.A.P. (Name, Address, Phone) INFO AT THE BOTTOM OF THE DESCRIPTION

- Use your keywords as tags and include the company name

- Choose the most appropriate screenshot

- Click "advanced settings" and add an address to the video

First, place your primary keywords in the title of the video as well as a description that includes the "HTTP://" before your web address.

In the description area, you can put in "We're a full-service personal injury firm. We serve these areas. This is our name, address, and phone number," but at the very top, you should have your website address, including the "HTTP://".

If you just put www.yourlawfirm.com, YouTube won't understand the link and it will show that it isn't clickable. If you put "HTTP://" in front of the link, it will be clickable and visitors will go straight to your page. They also get the link authority from having that link back to your website.

Choose the screenshot and add the video. Whenever you upload your video you can control your title and description, and add tags.

Titles Matter

Again, don't call your videos "your law firm name." Don't call it "personal injury law." Don't call it "auto accident." Call it "Your city + that service or case type," and then your law firm name. Title your videos the same way that somebody would search.

If it's your intro video, you might want to call it "your city + your primary service." For example, if you're a local Lakeland family law attorney - XYZ Law Firm." On the Child Custody page, "Lakeland Child Custody Attorney - XYZ Law Firm." It's crucial to title your videos properly to enable Google to locate them and include them in search results.

Next, in the description, add the link at the top. Your first objective is to include a link back to your homepage or to the specific page/practice area you discuss in your video. If it's the motorcycle accident page, put a link to that motorcycle accident page, and "http://yourlawfirm.com" -- make sure you include "HTTP://".

Below, add your tags. Within those tags you can put in your city law firm, your city auto accident attorney, your city premises liability law firm, and everything in between.

What Else Can You Do with Your Videos?

Now that you've updated your video and properly optimized it, your title is correct, and your description is posted, how can you leverage them? To receive the full benefits of the conversion component, post the videos to your website and social profiles, too.

What's the best way to do it? Copy the "embed code" and post the videos right on your site. The intro video should be embedded on the homepage and the service-specific videos should be posted on the appropriate sub-pages. We do this right within our YouTube channel or YouTube account.

Go to the video manager and find the list of all your videos. Choose the video you want to post on your website, click share, and select the embed option.

You will then be provided with a little piece of code, like the one to the right of my video image above. It is the specific code for that video, and it goes from I-frame to I-frame. If you are updating your website on your own, copy and paste the code right into your website's HTML. If you have a detached web manager, send the code off to them with details on where you want it posted.

Once the code is embedded in your HTML, it will show up on the page itself. That's your goal with these videos. And, of course, we don't have to limit ourselves to YouTube because there are multiple well-known video-sharing sites out there, including Vimeo and Dailymotion.

CHAPTER ELEVEN

Leverage Email Marketing to Connect with Your Clients on a Deeper Level, Get More Reviews and Social Media Followers, and Ultimately More Referral Business

Ever since email has existed, email marketing has existed. Email marketing is one of the oldest forms of advertising your business on the internet.

Although it gets a bad rap due to spam, it remains one of the most effective forms of marketing. When you do it right, email marketing produces phenomenal results. According to Campaign Monitor.com, the ROI for email marketing ranges between an incredible 3800% and 4400%: that's $38 to $44 for every dollar spent on an email marketing campaign. These stats pertain to all industries across the board.

Because of results like these, I am a big believer in email marketing. It's a powerful way to drive instant traffic to your website and make the telephone ring, but there is a right way and a wrong way to use it.

Did you know the easiest client is one that another client refers?

Every self-proclaimed marketing expert will tell you that's nothing new. With that said, many lawyers hardly ever market or keep in touch with their existing client base. Law firms will spend tens of thousands of dollars trying to get new customers but never think to market to the clients who already hired them.

Why is that? While I have many ideas, I suspect lawyers think that once a client is finished using their services, they will automatically refer their friends. This simply isn't true. Some lawyers don't want to bother their clients. The truth is clients want to hear from you and they want to be touched by your business. A monthly newsletter lets them know you care, you're still thinking about them and appreciate their business, and keeps you top-of-mind.

How Do You Start an Email Marketing Campaign?

The first thing you need is an email marketing platform like Mailchimp, Constant Contact, or Crazy Egg. Many CRMs provide a built-in email marketing platform as part of their system. Some of these platforms will blacklist you if you get a significant amount of unsubscribes and bounces. Only send email to your existing database and new potential clients whose email addresses you have acquired.

I understand the vital role email marketing plays in developing a connection with your clients. To begin, you must find a platform suited to your needs. Some of the popular email marketing services are paid services, with pricing based on the number of emails you send. They start at around $15.00 per month to send a couple of hundred emails.

Mailchimp

I have used Mailchimp in the past and like it for several reasons. It offers detailed tracking stats, the ability to post to your social networks, and a relatively user-friendly interface.

A user-friendly platform with a clean interface, Mailchimp provides many templates for its users. You can also add your own custom templates, which are a MUST for any law firm that wants to promote its brand. You need some knowledge of HTML but if you don't, you can hire a web designer to create one for you at a fairly inexpensive cost. Another benefit of Mailchimp? It's inexpensive, with plans starting at $10 per month.

Constant Contact

Constant Contact is another popular and often recommended platform. It's relatively easy to use and offers similar features to Mailchimp. However, it's a bit more complicated and expensive, with plans starting at $20 a month for 500 contacts or less.

Legal CRMs

Most generic CRMs today include an email newsletter option as part of the software. However, at the time of this printing, it appears most legal CRMs, including Clio, Lawyerist, CASEpeer, and Litify do not. Unless you're old-school, you most likely have an existing CRM; however, if the CRM you're using does not have an email newsletter option, you'll have to use an email newsletter platform.

Email list management is critical to longevity and referral business

There are now fee-based, useful email list management systems online. Your choice of system depends on your firm's size and mailing needs. Examples of EMSs include HUBSPOT, Capterra, FrontApp, Salesforce Marketing

Cloud, and others. If the variety of choices feels daunting and not necessarily something you want to spend time navigating, we can help you determine which one suits your needs.

How to Get Email Addresses

Lawyers ask me on a regular basis about how to get email addresses. It's not as easy as sending a letter in the USPS mail to anyone you desire. Reality check: just because they are your client and you have their email address doesn't mean you can send them anything if you don't have their permission.

It's certainly a fine line because you somehow already have their email address, and they have used your services before. Is it *really* considered spam? Technically, yes. You didn't ask them if you could send them a newsletter in email form. As a lawyer, you should include a paragraph in your retainer or engagement agreement that grants you permission to send newsletters electronically. Be sure to inform them that you are bound by client-attorney confidentiality and will never share or sell their information.

Explain that you send out tips, stories, and modifications to the law that may be relevant to them, specific to your area of law on a monthly basis, and would love to add them to your email list.

Remember, you want the opportunity to place your law firm's name in front of your clients every single month. You want to remain top-of-mind if one of their friends is looking for legal services like yours or if they run into another situation whereby they need you again. My favorite line from one of our family law clients is, "...and your second divorce is free."

Here's a perfect example of what could happen, even though it's not in the field of law. A pest control service provider came to my home several years ago. He did a good job and was very professional.

Four or five years later, I needed the services of the company again but I had lost his business card and could not remember the name of the company. I had to find another pest removal service. He lost the business because he never stayed in contact with me. He lost a huge job – $1,500.00 to be exact!

How many of you have experienced this exact same thing?

Start building your email list today.

Timing and Intent is Everything

First, what do I send? You must use the 80/20 rule: 80 percent good information and 20 percent sales. If all you send are emails about your practice areas and some other boring legalese, no one will ever read it. It's a perfect way to kill your list.

On the other hand, people love stories, especially if they involve overcoming hardship; for example, a heartwarming story about how you got custody of children, got someone out of jail who was unjustly charged, or won a significant award for someone who was injured are all excellent methods of creating the emotional bond you want to have with your clients. By sharing stories like these, you'll remain top-of-mind with them.

One other essential tip: always add reviews and testimonials, AND whenever possible, video testimonials you can embed into the newsletter. But keep the video short and sweet, under 90 seconds. Blogs are excellent for creating content that informs, but emails should be more personal and direct.

The frequency with which you send your emails is critical. One email per month, around the same time every month will ensure the client has your firm on their radar. It is important to commit to a date. More than once a month is too much and annoys people. Bombarding clients with emails is counterproductive.

I used to get three- to four emails a week from a company I purchased from in the past. These emails were 100 percent sales, sometimes sent several times a day. I HATED IT. Because it drove me crazy, I removed myself from that list very quickly. I have no doubt others did the same.

Get Legal

Make sure you have allowed customers an Opt-Out from receiving email messages at the bottom of every message. It must be easy for them to opt out because nothing is more annoying than receiving unwanted emails. If someone does not want to receive your messages, remove them from your list.

It does not mean they will never require your services again. They may be getting emails from too many sources and just want to clean out their email box. But let me caution you, if they want out and you keep sending emails to them, it's a sure-fire way to alienate them into never using your firm again.

Again, leverage email marketing as part of your overall internet marketing strategy. The most effective way to do it is by collecting the email addresses of all your clients and prospects. From there, use email marketing to get online reviews, engagement on your social media accounts, and remain top-of-mind as part of your strategy to obtain more repeat and referral business.

What is the Best Time to Send an Email Campaign?

These general email send-time tips are widely accepted by the email marketing community. They work well when you're starting off, but **be sure to read on and see why this won't always be the case.**

- **Day-time vs. Night-time.** While this one may be obvious, it's usually better to send out your email campaigns during the daytime. You know, when people are awake. Not asleep.

- **Mad Mondays.** The general consensus is that you should avoid sending out email blasts on Mondays. Why? People are already bummed out about the end of the weekend. They march into the office and are flooded with emails they've collected over the past few days. What's the first thing they do? Delete those emails of course!

- **Weekends.** Historically, weekends are the days when folks are out running errands and going on adventures. Weekends tend to have low open rates, so most marketers avoid them like the plague.

- **Fan Favorites: Tuesday, Wednesday, and Thursday.** Tuesday, Wednesday, and Thursday have traditionally been favorite days to send email campaigns, as email marketers seek to avoid the Monday angst and Friday's itchy feet. MailChimp confirms that Tuesday and Thursday are the two most popular days to send email newsletters.

CHAPTER TWELVE

Overview of Pay-Per-Click

If we revisit the **Online Marketing Plan** referenced in chapter one of this book, you will recall that the foundation of your Internet marketing plan should be focused on the organic, non-paid marketing efforts (Website, SEO, Google Maps, Social Media Marketing, Video Marketing, etc.).

Once you have a strong foundation, you should have the financial resources to invest in other paid online marketing initiatives.

Here's a brief recap of the paid online marketing options you should consider:

- Pay-Per-Click Marketing on Google AdWords and Microsoft Search (Yahoo & Bing)

- Paid online directory listings on sites like Martindale-Hubbell (martindale.com), Avvo.com, NOLO.com, Lawyers.com, and FindLaw.com

- Pay-Per-Lead and Lead Aggregators like NOLO.com, SuperLawyers.com, LawInfo.com, etc.

- Local Service Ads (LSA's)

Now, let's talk about what arguably may be the most powerful of these strategies (if done well) – Pay-Per-Click Marketing.

Pay-Per-Click Marketing (Google Ads AND Microsoft Advertising (Bing Ads) - How to maximize the profitability of your pay-per-click marketing efforts

In this chapter, we're going to review Pay-Per-Click Marketing to help you understand how it works, why it should be integrated into your overall strategy, where it can go wrong and right, and how you can implement it to develop an effective and timely marketing plan.

Why PPC Should Be Part of Your Overall Online Marketing Strategy

- Provides ability to rank on Page 1 if not top of the page for most any relevant and searched-enough keyword phrase (vs SEO which can take time - months, years, or even never) and is not subject to Google's organic algorithm changes

- Provides ability to control who does, and does not see your ads (through audience targeting, time of day / day of week, geography, negative keywords and more)

- Since it can be set up rather quickly: gives you rapid access to people looking for what you offer and awareness of your law firm and legal services you provide

- Excellent, ability to track results when all conversion tracking options are setup correctly

- Can yield a "force multiplier effect" and enhances your firm's credibility since if a prospect searches google and sees your Local Services (LSA) Ad, then sees your PPC ad, then sees your Google Business Profile (maps) listing then sees your organic (SEO) listing, you have more chances they will click on one of those, typically above and beyond the pure mathematical statistics of randomly clicking because consciously and unconsciously they see your brand so much on Page 1 of the search results page.

- PPC scales quickly once you've determined it's working

- Allows you to target prospects anywhere in the sales funnel, from the bottom (high commercial intent - likely ready to hire a firm) with a keyword like "divorce lawyer near me" to mid-funnel with a keyword like "how to prepare for divorce" to high in the funnel (discovery / awareness) for a keyword like "i am having trouble in my marriage" or "how to resolve conflict with my spouse" as well as YouTube and display network ads.

WHAT DOES PPC ACTUALLY DO?

First, unlike an SEO program, creating your website, building links, and establishing the right on-page optimization – a process that takes time to yield a return – PPC can generate results quickly (when done properly and well of course – let's assume that is the case moving forward). Rather than paying dividends in many months, with PPC advertising, once you set up your campaign, you will start to see your ads serve within hours to just a couple of days.

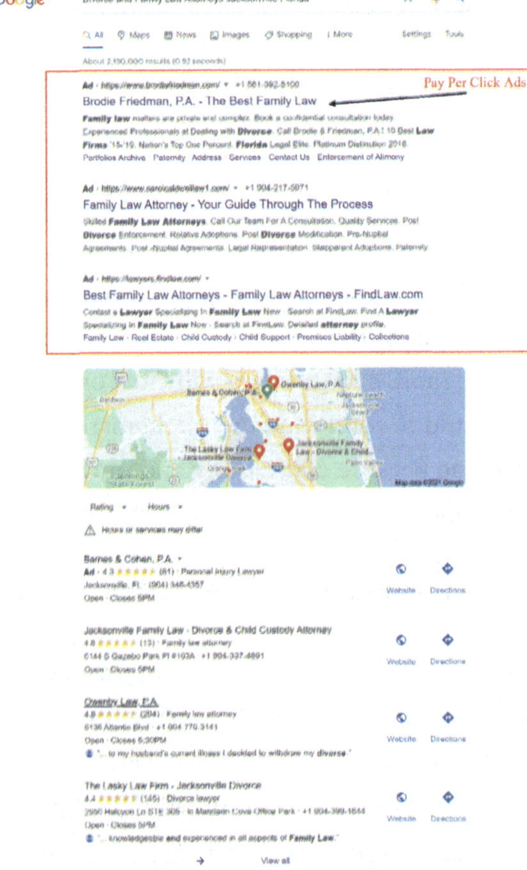

We have already examined the differences between the paid listings, the organic listings, and the map listings. To use an example to highlight the importance of leveraging PPC during peak times for your business, consider a flower shop. A week or so before Valentine's Day, when couples seek the perfect gift for their Valentine, the owner of the flower shop can use PPC.

Why? People are researching flower shops in their area more often than an average day of the year. For a florist that wants to show up as often as possible when someone is looking for their services, a pay-per-click ad that displays somewhere at the top of the search results page, an organic listing on the map, and appearing lower on the page in the organic section magnifies their visibility. It affords the florist an opportunity to show up in multiple places, significantly improving the chances of a potential client clicking on their ad, as opposed to competitors who show up less on page or on page 2 or 3 of the search results. In this scenario, a pay-per-click campaign gives the flower shop owner an additional placeholder on the search engines on page one, along with the opportunity to show up for words that they may not show up for in their organic SEO efforts.

Beyond just keywords, in addition to time of day and day of week targeting and/or "bid adjustments", you can do the same with locations, devices, demographics such as gender or home owner vs renter, as well as other audiences both broader (affinity audiences) and more specific (in-marketing audiences), with the former being determined over a longer term time frame and the latter being determined for a relatively short time frame.

A bid adjustment since we just mentioned it, allows you to potentially show your ad higher or lower to people based on how much you are willing to pay for a click. For example, you can create a bid adjustment such that if the user doing a search for your keyword is also identified by Google as having achieved an "advanced college degree", you can decide to pay up to 20% more per click when that criterion is met. By the same token you could decide to pay some percentage less like -30%. Your "Max CPC" (Maximum Cost Per Click) is a significant factor in the "Ad Rank" formula which determines how high or low your ad actually appears in the search results (and even if it appears at all).

The Pay Per Click Sites

What are the Pay Per Click "Sites"?

The three largest PPC services are Google Ads, Microsoft Ads and Facebook Ads. Numerous other platforms exist that can provide niche or much lower volume lead potential such as LinkedIn Ads, Yelp Ads and various Social Media Marketing (SMM) sites. The two-search engine focused PPC sites are Google Ads (formerly known as Google AdWords) which can be found at https://ads.google.com, and Microsoft Ads (formerly known as Bing Ads), which can be found at https://ads.microsoft.com and their primary focus is form them to show your ads on their primary search engine (google.com for Google and bing.com for Microsoft).

In addition to your ads showing on their owned sites (for Google beyond google.com think YouTube.com often considered the "2nd largest search engine" and for Microsoft beyond Bing.com think MSN.com, Live.com and others), these both also have their own network of partner sites, so when you pay for a PPC ad campaign on Google's search network, you have the option (by default it is selected for new campaigns) of also appearing on

Google's "Search Partner Network" which are sites vetted and monitored by Google for quality. Google does not disclose exactly which sites are in its Search Partner Network, however, in the past this has included sites like Amazon and Ask.com. While advertisers are able to opt-out of showing ads on the Search Partner Network, my experience is the traffic quality while is just fine although the volume of traffic is small so we allow most campaigns to show ads on Google's Search Partner Network.

When you get on the Microsoft search network, you're getting access to a larger number of other sites, but are of suspect quality in my experience so we opt-out of their partner search network.

There are, however, a variety of reasons to consider adding Microsoft Ads to your PPC strategy. The most obvious is additional traffic and lead potential of approximately 10% of what Google provides yet in most campaigns pay less than half of what you'd pay per click for Google. Lead quality with Microsoft Ads can vary. Some of our campaigns show higher quality leads, while others show lower. Ultimately you should test, track and evaluate. Microsoft owns LinkedIn and has integrated data from LinkedIn's user base to allow advertisers to refine your targeting by job function, industry and even company through bid adjustments (but not solely through inclusion or exclusion).

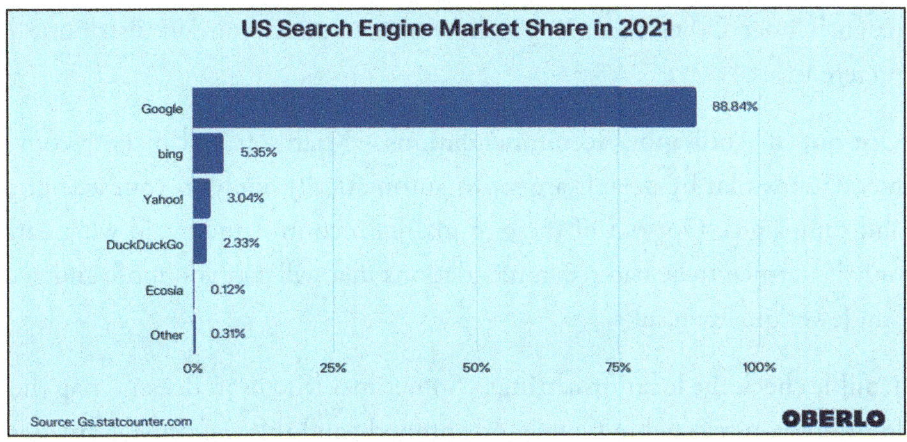

You can see in the chart above it clearly shows that Google is the dominant search engine with no serious competition. Therefore, most advertisers only focus on Google which is precisely why adding Microsoft Ads can be beneficial. The effort to setup campaigns in Microsoft Ads is dramatically reduced by simply importing your campaigns from Google Ads.

Pro Tip: When first establishing your account and campaigns with Microsoft Ads, I recommend the following:

Turn off scheduled/automatic imports from Google Ads - Once you've imported the campaigns you want from your Google Ads account the first time (I recommend only importing standard search campaigns and NOT "specialty" search campaigns like Smart, Discovery, etc. nor importing Display nor YouTube campaigns), you must turn off the setting for scheduled imports otherwise any work you do on your campaigns will be overwritten repeatedly.

Cut Bids and Budgets by about 50% - No need to pay as much as Google when there's much less competition. Cut your daily budget and CPC bids by at least half to start. It usually won't affect your visibility yet you'll better ensure you don't spend more than necessary.

Only show ads on Microsoft owned sites, Yahoo & AOL - This is a specific setting under you'll find when you show all the ad groups within a campaign. Under Other changes, you'll be able to select your ad distribution preferences.

Opt-out of Auto-apply recommendations - Microsoft will make recommendations that by default are set to automatically apply to your account and campaigns. Opt-out of these to maintain control and avoid what can only be termed to be bad recommendations that will cost you more and get you fewer quality results.

Double check the location settings - Sometimes Microsoft doesn't map the locations you selected in Google Ads properly and this can cause a broader geographical targeting. I've seen this default to the entire country which as you may imagine can be a costly mistake if you don't change it.

UNDERSTANDING THE GOOGLE ADWORDS AUCTION PROCESS

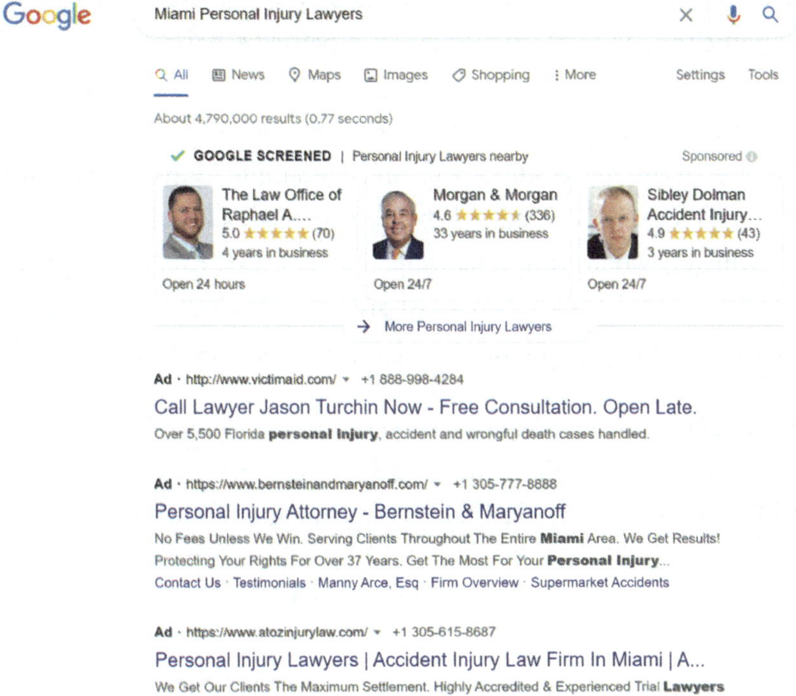

HOW GOOGLE ADS WORKS

In the simplest sense, you're paying on a per-click basis and can choose your keywords and the locations of the searchers for which you want your ad to appear. For example, personal injury lawyer in Miami, personal injury lawyer near me, local personal injury lawyer. As you pick those phrases, you bid and pay on a per-click basis. Suppose you're bidding on the keyword "San Antonio Family Lawyer" and there are many family lawyers in that city who want to rank for that keyword.

While it might seem like if you are willing to pay $22.00/click (called your Max CPC where CPC is Cost Per Click) and your competitor says that they'll pay $25.00/click, their ad will be above yours because they are willing to pay more. However, the reality is there are other factors involved to where it's actually possible for your ad to appear higher than a competitor ad even though you are willing to pay (and would end up paying) less for that click! The main point though is that you pay on a per-click basis, and you are bidding against the competitors in the auction to determine (partially) how your ad will rank for your keyword. It's an auction, kind of like eBay except the quality of your ad and landing page and for simplicity purposes, with how well your Google Ads account is being managed, all factor into your "Ad Rank" which is where your ad appears in the search results compared to your competition. That said, firms that are willing to bid enough higher than the rest do tend to rank higher but that's not the main factor.

With that foundational understanding, we can now explain why so many law firm PPC campaigns fail to meet expectations or fail to produce a positive ROI or in some cases even fail to even any get viable leads at all.

WHY SO MANY PAY PER CLICK CAMPAIGNS "FAIL"

You might be thinking, "Josh, you just told me PPC is an excellent way to attract potential clients, and now you're saying that most campaigns fail!" I'm going to explain what people do wrong and then show you what to do right to better ensure your campaign's success.

There are many things that can influence a PPC campaign's results. Sometimes even one element can significantly drag down results, other times, it's the combination of multiple elements that may be underperforming individually but add up to a meaningful amount of wasted click spend, erosion of lead quality and ultimately fewer leads / clients.

Some of the primary reasons I've seen for why a law firm fails to see the desired result from PPC include but are not limited to:

- Poor keyword selection
- Wrong use of match types for the situation
- Using standard broad match for keywords (unless you have a very, very specific strategy and constraining variables in place)
- Not doing ongoing search term maintenance and excluding any non-relevant or ambiguous intent / low commercial intent / informational research keywords
- Combining too many varied keywords into one ad group (you would not want to have keywords like "child custody lawyer", "divorce lawyer" and "family law attorney" all in the same Ad Group. You would want to separate them out, customize the ad copy and then send to different landing pages with each page specific to each type of case.)
- Little to no use of negative keywords (more is usually better)
- Poor use of negative keywords (not using the right ones)
- Ad copy is unremarkable, generic and/or looks like everyone else's ads
- Not using Ad Extensions: site links, callouts, call extensions, location extensions, structured snippets and image extensions. While there are some others, they typically don't apply or aren't a good option for most law firms. Ad Extensions augment your ads, essentially bulking them up and allowing you to better differentiate yourself from other ads

- Landing page(s) are poor converters, not relevant enough or even not used (and therefore visitors are just sent to the home page)
- Geographical targeting and settings for campaigns are improperly set
- Using the wrong bidding strategy, wrong parameters for a bidding strategy and/or blindly trusting automated bidding and not monitoring KPIs
- Audiences are not being used or bid modifiers are not being utilized for desirable audiences and better ad positioning in search results
- Not considering the ability to exclude or CPC bid adjust certain demographics (age, average Household Income, level of education, home ownership, etc.)
- Blindly accepting Google's recommendations in the Recommendations tab within the Google Ads account or blindly listening to a Google Ads representative's advice (not all recommendations are appropriate for every account). Beware of the term "Google best practices" when applied too uniformly. A best practice for one set of goals is not necessarily a best practice for a different set of goals or type of law
- Combining networks into same campaign (Search Network campaigns should be separate from Display Network campaigns)
- Not excluding mobile apps and poor performing sites in Display Network campaigns (fraud does exist in the Display Network and doing this helps reduce it in many cases, we typically exclude ALL mobile apps)

- Lack of, or improper conversion tracking (this sometimes means your campaign is actually working but it's not tracked well enough to know)

And yes, there's more but the above are the biggest ones

Also, beware that Google continues to loosen up what search terms match your campaign keywords. A search term is what someone actually typed into google whereas a keyword is the keyword in your campaign. For example, you may have the keyword "car accident lawyer" but google will show your ad for "show for a term like "car accident yesterday on the news" which clearly is not someone looking for a lawyer but instead is an information search. So depending on which "match type" is selected for each keyword in your campaigns, your ad may show for non-relevant searches or more informational / research phrases. This is one of several areas many law firms waste click spend.

MARKETING TESTING AS APPLIED TO PPC ACCOUNTS

Testing is a staple of marketing. However, for law firms with somewhat smaller click budgets (Under $2K/mo), it can take quite a while to accumulate a statistically valid sample size of data for which to make decisions that auto accident attorney near me". That doesn't seem too bad but more and more, you are likely to have a high confidence level of being correct.

For example, if you have 4 main types of cases, and you create 4 campaigns, one for each. Then each campaign, all things being equal, would have a budget of $500/mo. If within each campaign, you had two different ad groups (groups of keyword terms), then each ad group would have a $250/month budget (if equal). And if you had 2 ads in each ad group, then that's $125 per month per ad. If your clicks were $25 each on average, then again, if clicks and budget were spread equally across all components of the account, you would get 5 clicks per ad, per ad group. In 1 entire year, each ad would see 60 clicks. Trying to determine a winner and loser amongst just 2 ads with only 60 clicks each is not going to be as accurate as if they had a lot more clicks. And if you had 4 ads instead of 2 in each ad group, or 2 ads going to 1 landing page and another 2 ads going to another landing page, you can see that it can literally take 1-2 years to get enough data to base a decision on regarding which is the winner or loser. With bigger budgets or low enough cost per click, etc. the math changes of course to where you may need less time. The point here is that most accounts do not warrant constant changes. It takes time to generate enough data to determine performance.

Another item related to testing is that Google Ads has a setting for Ad Rotation. One is "optimize: show best performing ads" and the other is "rotate evenly". When you leave it to Google by using the first setting, Google is doing the testing. So there's really nothing for you to test! Also, Google currently allows for 2 types of ads in standard Search campaigns: RSA's and ETA's. RSA's are Responsive Search Ads and ETA's are Expanded Text Ads. The RSA's allow for up to 15 headlines of 30 characters each and up to 4 description lines of up to 90 characters each. Google will mix and match various headline and description line permutations and shows the ones it deems relevant to a particular search and/or is performing the best. So with RSA's, you aren't really testing, Google is. With that many headlines and descriptions, each unique combination will not add up to any significant total any time soon if the account budget is a few grand. Currently RSA's do not provide advertisers with highly granular data, so it's actually hard to know what combinations perform best.

ADVANCED PPC STRATEGIES

Actually, some of the things I've shared already in this chapter is relatively advanced as compared to many of the PPC accounts we assume from another agency or audit when managed by another agency. That said, Google Ads continues to get more complicated and simpler at the same time. I know, it sounds contradictory and in a way it is! Google keeps adding more capabilities and features, campaign types, etc. It also continues to automate and use Artificial Intelligence (AI) machine learning to generate better results for advertisers who let Google "take the wheel and drive" so to speak.

The keys to the constantly changing PPC landscape are to of course keep up with the changes and latest features but also to test them. That's one of the many benefits of working with a competent digital marketing agency, since an agency has knowledge, experience, and insights across many different accounts, each one can test different things. Therefore, your law firm benefits from that accumulated knowledge.

LANDING PAGES AND A "CALL TO ACTION" ARE CRITICAL TO SUCCESSFUL MARKETING CAMPAIGNS ONLINE

Typically, businesses set up only one campaign, using only one ad group for all services, whether it's personal injury lawyer, personal injury, slip-and-fall lawyer, medical malpractice, truck accidents, etc. instead of different ad groups for each type of service. There are no specific text ads and no landing pages for those ad groups and groups of keywords.

You end up with the same landing page and the same text ad, whether your client typed in "personal injury lawyer, bicycle accident, slip-and-fall attorney, medical malpractice, personal injury attorney, etc." in the search engine.

Whatever they typed into the search engine was likely specific, and should match up to a specific page, but that doesn't happen. Instead, it all goes to the home page. With this strategy, not only will your campaign convert poorly, your cost-per-click will also be higher. I will explain why later in this chapter.

The other reason why most pay-per-click campaigns fail is that there isn't a strong **call-to-action on the landing page**. That means you just paid $5.00 or $9.00 to attract a potential client to your website and the page isn't even compelling because it doesn't tell the consumer what to do next.

By remembering these common reasons for the failure of pay-per-click campaigns, you can better prepare and set yourself up for success in the execution of your pay-per-click marketing.

Understanding the PPC Auction Process

Let's talk about how the PPC Auction process works. It's not as simple as the highest bidder winning. It's much more complicated.

Google must feature the most relevant results because their endgame is to ensure that people keep using their search engine over the competition. This is how they can maintain their traffic. Google can maintain its usage and that 80 percent market share but can also run AdWords and make billions of dollars per year. Ultimately it all comes down to relevancy.

The second they sacrifice relevancy for dollars is the second they start to become less of a player in their market. Therefore, Google had to figure out a way to make their pay-per-click program grow around relevancy. That's why they established the quality score. They must ensure that the person or company that has more relevance gets a higher quality score and, as result, can have a lower cost per click.

Here's how I like to explain it: if I go to Google and type in "BMW," obviously I am looking for a BMW dealer or information about BMW. Mercedes could say, "That's our demographic, too. If someone types in

BMW, they're looking for a high-end vehicle. They are probably in the market to buy. Why don't I bid on the word BMW?" Of course, they can. However, the person that searched BMW isn't looking for Mercedes. Mercedes could say, "I'll pay $25.00 for everybody that clicks on me when they search 'BMW'."

But BMW might say, "That's my brand and I am going to compete for it; however, I am not going to spend $25.00 for every click on my own brand. I'll pay a dollar for every click." Based on the quality score, Google may decide to serve BMW because it's in the best interest of the person researching the brand, the consumer. It's also in the best interest of overall relevancy. That's how the quality score works.

Quality score is really driven by three core components:

1. Click-Through Rate
2. Ad Relevance
3. Landing Page Experience

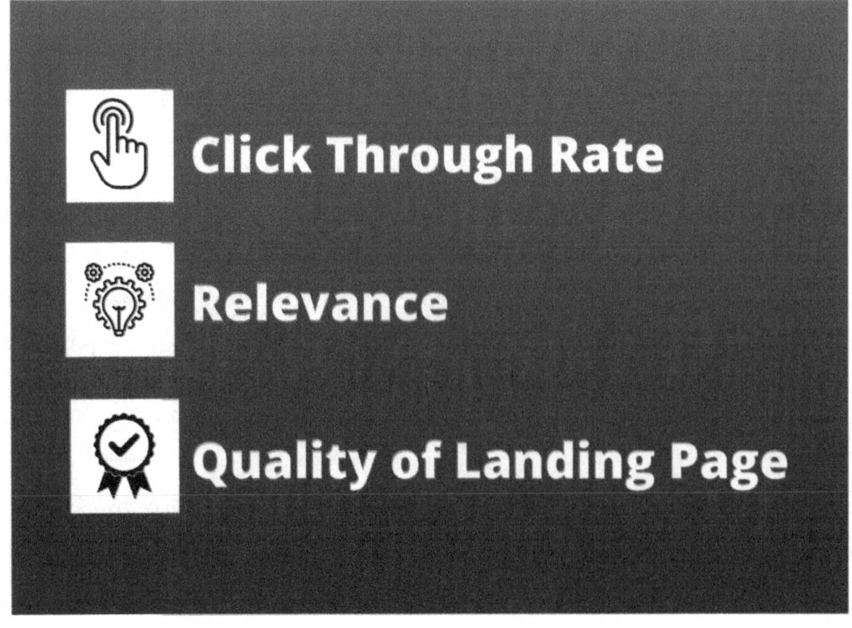

As somebody conducts a search and your website shows up on the page in the pay-per-click section, Google is tracking what percentage of those people saw your ad and wound up clicking through.

That's one of the primary metrics they analyze. If your ad is relevant, speaks to the person's needs, and compels them enough to click through, Google just made more per click. They will be more willing to give you a higher quality score because you've got a better click-through rate.

Relevancy is another major factor. How relevant is your text ad to the keyword your potential client typed? For example, if they type in "truck accident," and your text ad reads: "We're the most experienced truck accident attorneys in the Dallas area," versus "We're the most experienced truck accident attorneys in the Dallas area and we represent clients who have suffered truck accidents in the Dallas area."

Which do you think is more relevant to the customer? Google wants their search results to be as applicable as possible. They're looking at your click-through rate, the relevancy of your text ad to your keywords, and the quality of your landing page.

If your landing page (the page to which you drive people) doesn't match up with what the person just clicked based on your text ad, or if that landing page doesn't have a strong call-to-action and the person quickly returns to the search engine, that signals to Google that you were not relevant. This will result in a quality score reduction.

Better Quality Score =
Lower Cost Per Click for Top Positions

By having a higher quality score, you can bid lower and still achieve the top position. This is where you can win in the pay-per-click marketing game because a better-quality score results in a lower cost-per-click for those who hold the top positions.

Again, here are the reasons most pay-per-click campaigns fail:

- You only set up one ad group
- You had the opportunity to create a separate ad group for each one of your practice areas, but you did not use a specific text ad that compels someone to click and improve your click-through rate
- You don't have a strong call-to-action that matches up with what the consumer was looking for
- You're not going to have a high click-through rate, relevancy, or an applicable landing page

All of these issues result in a lower quality score.

You'll end up paying more per click. PPC marketing is fiercely competitive. If you're paying more per click, you're not going to be able to spend that much because you won't be getting enough calls to generate a return on investment.

The visual representation of this would be like setting up one AdWords campaign for each one of these services (lawyer, family lawyer, family law firm, child custody, divorce, dental braces, etc.) and landing people on your home page. That is a recipe for disaster. Don't do it.

HOW TO SET UP YOUR PPC CAMPAIGN FOR SUCCESS

Let's talk about how to position your pay-per-click campaign for success.

What can you do to ensure the highest probability of success in your pay-per-click campaign? For starters, set up ad groups based on the specific groups of services that you offer (we're going to map this out using a variety of businesses as an example).

Write compelling text ads that are relevant to your specific keywords or services. Then, link your ads to the specific pages on your site rather than the home page. But the specific pages on your site that talk about that service should have a strong call-to-action combined with an offer.

What ad groups should you use? What ad groups do you need to set up for your business? Using a dental clinic company as an example:

What Ad Groups should you use?

- Dental Braces
- Invisalign
- Cosmetic Dentistry
- Family Dentistry
- Teeth Cleaning
- Periodontics

If you are a personal injury attorney, you must include "personal injury attorney" for the general, "I need a personal injury attorney," or "I'm looking for a personal injury attorney" search. That is not specific, but you should have something for that more general search. However, you should also include "auto accident attorney", "car accident attorney", truck accident attorney" for the person who types in "auto accident attorney," "car accident attorney" "truck accident attorney," etc. You want to group those keywords together and provide information for that.

We could go a lot deeper than this, but you should have an idea of what specific types of ad groups you need to set up based on the areas of law that you practice. From there, you want to write a specific text ad that speaks to that group of keywords.

Then, drive them to a landing page on your website that has a compelling call-to-action, provides what they were looking for, and mirrors what your text ad said. Review the template below:

- Pick your list of keywords
- Write a specific text ad that matches up with what those people are looking for
- Drive them to a landing page on your website

Make sure that you've got compelling content on that landing page that emphasizes what they were looking for and prompts them into action, ideally with some type of offer as a free download, to keep them on your page and prevent them from looking around.

In addition, I highly recommend a little-known trick: if you have at least five major keywords repeating on your landing page, Google can crawl it, which automatically increases your quality score.

Wedding showcase AdWords example

Let's look at the bridal showcase example. For an upcoming bridal showcase, in general, you're going to have the following keywords:

- Bridal expo
- Wedding expo
- Bridal show
- Wedding show
- Wedding showcase

- Upcoming bridal showcase

These are the keywords that go into this general bridal showcase ad group. Your text ad should speak to that search.

> "Connecting Brides and Grooms with Top Long Island Wedding Professionals. February 10, 11, 12"

You want to pull on the psychological triggers. Are they looking for affordability? Are they looking for quick service? Typically, they are.

Then, drive them to the URL on your site that is specifically targeted at the bridal showcase, Yourcompany.com/bridalshowcase. Get them to the page that talks about that specific service.

There are a lot of things you can do on the landing page, but you want to make sure that you tap into that psychological trigger.

MEET TOP LONG ISLAND WEDDING PROFESSIONALS

Free Admission

Brides + Grooms + Family & Friends

Live DJ Showcase at All Shows

Monday, February 10, Marriott Uniondale,

After Hours Entertainment

Tuesday, February 11, Marriott Melville, Variety Music

Wednesday, February 12, Clarion Hotel, Ronkonkoma,

After Hours Entertainment

Live Fashion show hosted by Princess Bridals

Meet with 35 to 40 Wedding Experts at each show featuring Photography, Videography, Wedding Gowns, Caterers and Reception Sites, Limousines,

Flowers, DJ's with Musical Performers, Medications, Invitations, Cakes, Tuxedo's, Hair and Makeup Salons, Financial & Insurance Planners, Real Estate & Mortgage Experts, Photo Booth Companies and More! Meet Top Wedding Professionals and get pricing information for your wedding. At Long Island Bridal Expo, Everything for Your Wedding Under One Roof!

Talk about why they should choose you, not the competition, and provide a link to a page where they can see some external resources.

What does the BBB say about you? What reviews do you have on Yelp.com? Give them information that instills confidence in your organization's credibility and reliability.

Then, provide a strong offer with a call-to-action: "Get $50 off your service by referencing the coupon below. Call now!: If you have the capabilities built into your website, consider linking them to a form where they can choose to type in their name and phone number to schedule the service on the spot.

Wedding DJ

This is a well-crafted ad group specifically for the Wedding DJ keywords.

Let's look at Wedding DJ keywords. The consumer typed in wedding DJ, sound DJ, leading wedding DJ, best DJ for a wedding, top-rated DJs, party DJ, etc. These people have an immediate need for wedding DJ services. Group those keywords together, save it as an ad group, and create a specific text ad for that.

"The Most Tasteful, Talented and Experienced DJs In New England Since 1983. Build Your Event Today. Quick, Free Custom Quotes. Multiple Wedding Services."

You say just what they want to hear. They've got an emergency and you're entering the conversation that's already going on in their head. You're offering them some type of incentive to do business with you.

Again, you drive them to the Wedding DJ Services page on your website (Example: www.yourcompany.com/wedding_dj. Then provide content that speaks to that specific situation.

"New England's Top-Rated Wedding DJ!!"

"Since 1983, we have set new standards in quality and style for wedding DJ entertainment in New England. For over 30 years, we have been the most respected and recognized name in the disc jockey business, offering unmatched service and professionalism to the New England area including Connecticut, Rhode Island, New York, & Massachusetts."

Restate that value proposition. Show them reviews. Give them an offer, "Get $50 off your next DJ hire by referencing the coupon below. Call now."

When you set up your ad groups this way, you'll achieve high ad relevance, a higher click-through ratio, and better conversions because you're speaking directly to the consumers' needs. You are also giving them a call-to-action and maybe even a special incentive to choose you right at that moment.

If you are a wedding photographer and the person typed in any type of wedding photography term, you must have a specific AdGroup for that and a slightly different approach.

You can pick a wedding photographer, best wedding photographer, party and event photographer, etc.

"Capture the moments at your party, shower, corporate networking, or other celebrations. Visit my site to see my Portfolio, and call/email for a quote."

Drive them to the wedding photography page on your website. On that page, speak to the specific search.

"We offer professional digital photography. From Weddings to Birthdays and just about any event, we will capture the sights of your special event in an unobtrusive Wedding Ceremony manner so that you can enjoy your event without having to deal with a pushy photographer."

In some cases, you will be dealing with services that have a longer purchasing cycle.

Car repair, for example. If it's general repair or a lift kit installation, car hail damage repair, or even remodeling, customers will not necessarily pick up and call right at that moment.

They might just be in the researching process. For these types of services, offer them something for free, such as a free auto body inspection or 10 things to know before you remodel your existing car. Provide a lead capture form, where they can enter their name and their email address to download those guides.

This enables you to catch people when they're in the first stages of their evaluation process. Send them a well-crafted guide that talks about what they should be thinking about and sets the buying criteria in your favor.

Educate and Engage

Why would they want to choose your company versus the competition? What things must they be made aware of? Must they ensure that they're dealing with somebody who is licensed and insured? Do they need to confirm that they're dealing with somebody with vast experience in auto repairing, as opposed to just offering basic car repair service?

In that guide, you can really position yourself and educate them in a way that will make them want to utilize your services. You can also use email marketing to send them messages over time. If they're at the beginning of a car repair or car remodeling project, you do your best to catch them early. Maybe it's going to be six months before they decide to make the final decision or to move forward with any type of project.

Because you got their email you could send them one email per week for the next six months. They're going to get something new from you once a week. Nothing annoying, but "Here's an update, here's another thing, here's another interesting concept you can look at".

When they do get to the point that they are ready to move forward, they've seen you so many times and you've added so much value that they have no choice but to choose your company. You've made the decision easy for them.

This is a way to position yourself better for the longer purchase cycle projects, so you can capture more leads and convert them into customers.

AdWords Setup Best Practices

Here are some best practices when you get into Google AdWords (google.com/AdWords).

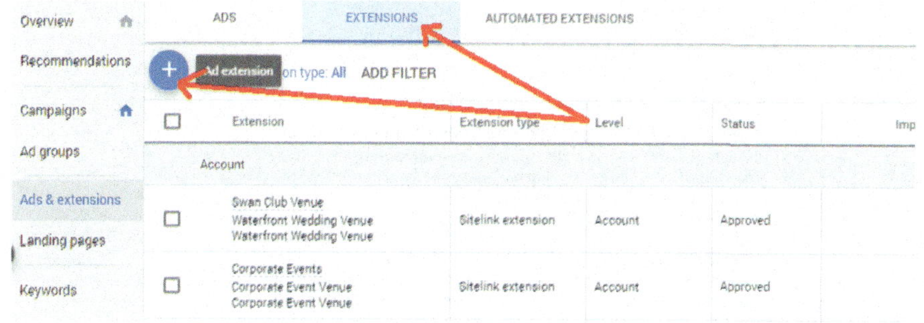

First, set up an extension with your address.

In chapter one, we showed you how to create your Google Map listing and optimize it to rank in the Google Map. Use the same Gmail account you claimed your map listing with on Google AdWords, so that you can come into extensions and add your address as an extension. This allows you to add your address and a direct link to your Google Places listing in your search.

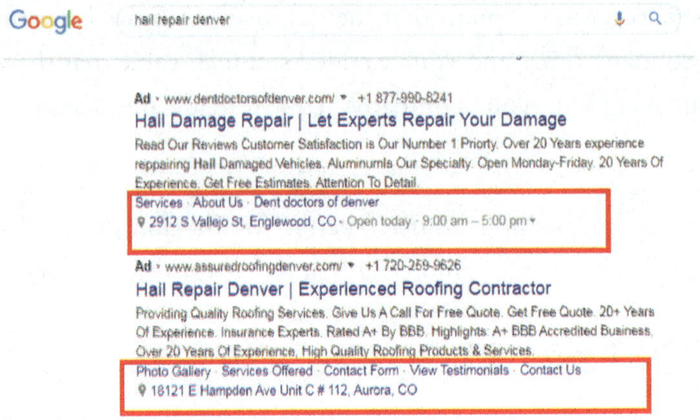

Google hail repair denver

Ad · www.dentdoctorsofdenver.com/ ▾ +1 877-990-8241
Hail Damage Repair | Let Experts Repair Your Damage
Read Our Reviews Customer Satisfaction is Our Number 1 Priorty. Over 20 Years experience reppairing Hail Damaged Vehicles. Aluminumls Our Specialty. Open Monday-Friday. 20 Years Of Experience. Get Free Estimates. Attention To Detail.
Services · About Us · Dent doctors of denver
2912 S Vallejo St, Englewood, CO - Open today · 9:00 am – 5:00 pm ▾

Ad · www.assuredroofingdenver.com/ ▾ +1 720-259-9626
Hail Repair Denver | Experienced Roofing Contractor
Providing Quality Roofing Services. Give Us A Call For Free Quote. Get Free Quote. 20+ Years Of Experience. Insurance Experts. Rated A+ By BBB. Highlights: A+ BBB Accredited Business, Over 20 Years Of Experience, High Quality Roofing Products & Services.
Photo Gallery · Services Offered · Contact Form · View Testimonials · Contact Us
18121 E Hampden Ave Unit C # 112, Aurora, CO

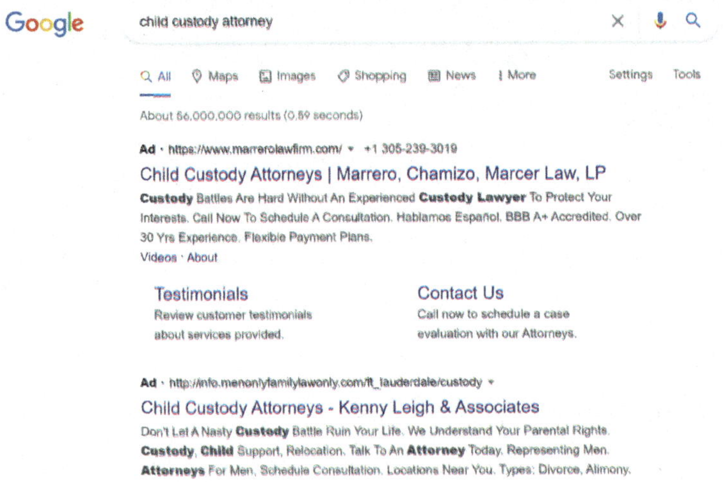

Google child custody attorney

All · Maps · Images · Shopping · News · More · Settings · Tools

About 56,000,000 results (0.59 seconds)

Ad · https://www.marrerolawfirm.com/ ▾ +1 305-239-3019
Child Custody Attorneys | Marrero, Chamizo, Marcer Law, LP
Custody Battles Are Hard Without An Experienced **Custody Lawyer** To Protect Your Interests. Call Now To Schedule A Consultation. Hablamos Español. BBB A+ Accredited. Over 30 Yrs Experience. Flexible Payment Plans.
Videos · About

Testimonials
Review customer testimonials about services provided.

Contact Us
Call now to schedule a case evaluation with our Attorneys.

Ad · http://info.menonlyfamilylawonly.com/ft_lauderdale/custody ▾
Child Custody Attorneys - Kenny Leigh & Associates
Don't Let A Nasty **Custody** Battle Ruin Your Life. We Understand Your Parental Rights. **Custody**, **Child** Support, Relocation. Talk To An **Attorney** Today. Representing Men. **Attorneys** For Men. Schedule Consultation. Locations Near You. Types: Divorce, Alimony.

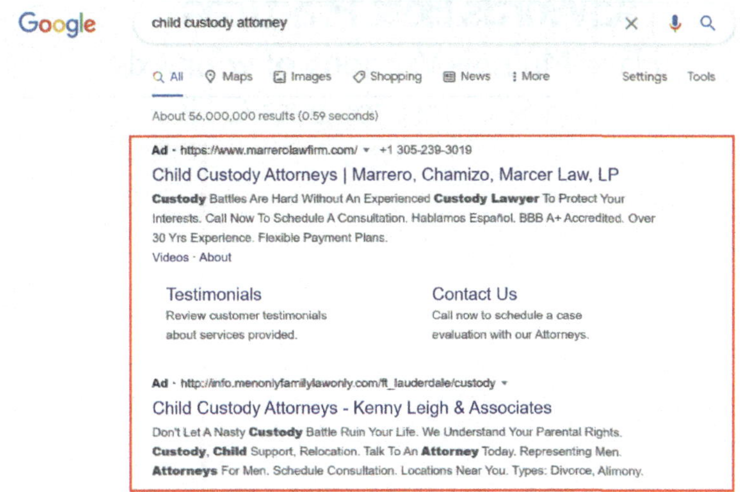

In the screenshot above, you can see the ads for two Child Custody Attorneys. Not only do they have their text ad, but they've also got additional extensions on the ad with important site links, a link to their Google Places listing, and their address. Notice how it sets off these two ads a little more than the others. Consider taking the time to set up your AdWords extensions. I highly recommend it.

Have Multiple Text Ads for Each AdGroup and Run Split Tests

The other best practice is to have multiple text ads for every one of your ad groups. It enables you to split-test, see each of your ads, and determine which one is converting better.

For example, split-test by looking at these two ads for Steak Restaurant. They're just different variations of the same messaging that will get equal share. If there are one thousand impressions, you could distribute 500 to one and 500 to the other.

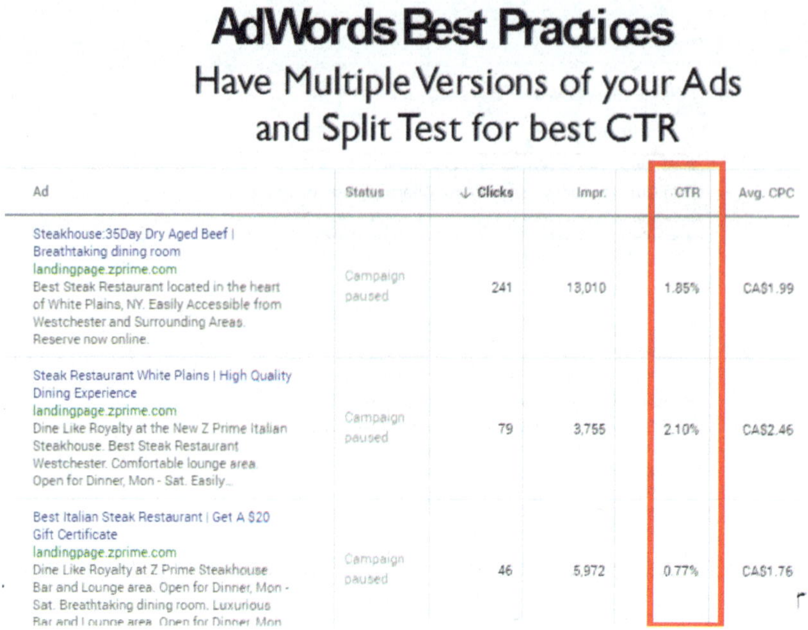

AdWords Best Practices

Have Multiple Versions of your Ads and Split Test for best CTR

Ad	Status	↓ Clicks	Impr.	CTR	Avg. CPC
Steakhouse:35Day Dry Aged Beef | Breathtaking dining room landingpage.zprime.com Best Steak Restaurant located in the heart of White Plains, NY. Easily Accessible from Westchester and Surrounding Areas. Reserve now online.	Campaign paused	241	13,010	1.85%	CA$1.99
Steak Restaurant White Plains | High Quality Dining Experience landingpage.zprime.com Dine Like Royalty at the New Z Prime Italian Steakhouse. Best Steak Restaurant Westchester. Comfortable lounge area. Open for Dinner, Mon - Sat. Easily...	Campaign paused	79	3,755	2.10%	CA$2.46
Best Italian Steak Restaurant | Get A $20 Gift Certificate landingpage.zprime.com Dine Like Royalty at Z Prime Steakhouse Bar and Lounge area. Open for Dinner, Mon - Sat. Breathtaking dining room. Luxurious Bar and Lounge area. Open for Dinner, Mon	Campaign paused	46	5,972	0.77%	CA$1.76

By split testing, you can determine which one had a higher click-through rate. With that information, you can drop out the lower performing ad and create a new one.

At the end of the month, compare the two ads to see which one performed better. Keep doing it consistently to improve your click-through ratios. Remember, better click-through rates will drive more traffic, but they will also give you a higher quality score. Over time, this will reduce your cost-per-click and make it more profitable for you in the long term.

Pay Attention to Average Position

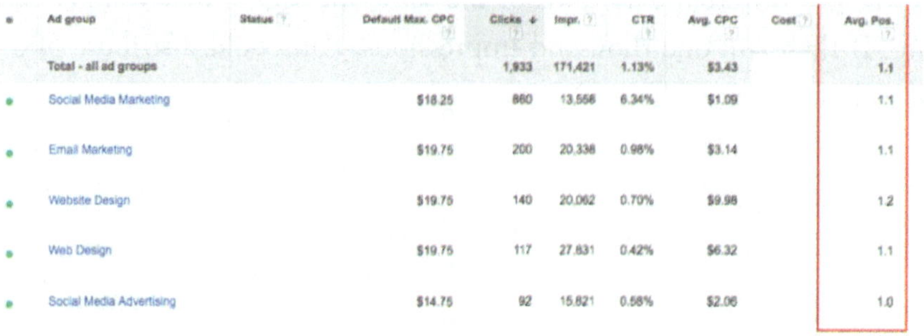

●	Ad group	Status	Default Max. CPC	Clicks ↓	Impr.	CTR	Avg. CPC	Cost	Avg. Pos.
	Total - all ad groups			1,933	171,421	1.13%	$3.43		1.1
●	Social Media Marketing		$18.25	860	13,556	6.34%	$1.09		1.1
●	Email Marketing		$19.75	200	20,338	0.98%	$3.14		1.1
●	Website Design		$19.75	140	20,062	0.70%	$9.98		1.2
●	Web Design		$19.75	117	27,831	0.42%	$6.32		1.1
●	Social Media Advertising		$14.75	92	15,821	0.58%	$2.06		1.0

Pay attention to your average position in your Google AdWords campaign. These available settings make it simple to analyze the data. In the report above, you can see what position is being maintained. The average position is highlighted. This is based on the quality score and the average cost per click. You want to maintain a top-four position on the major search engines in your pay-per-click marketing campaign.

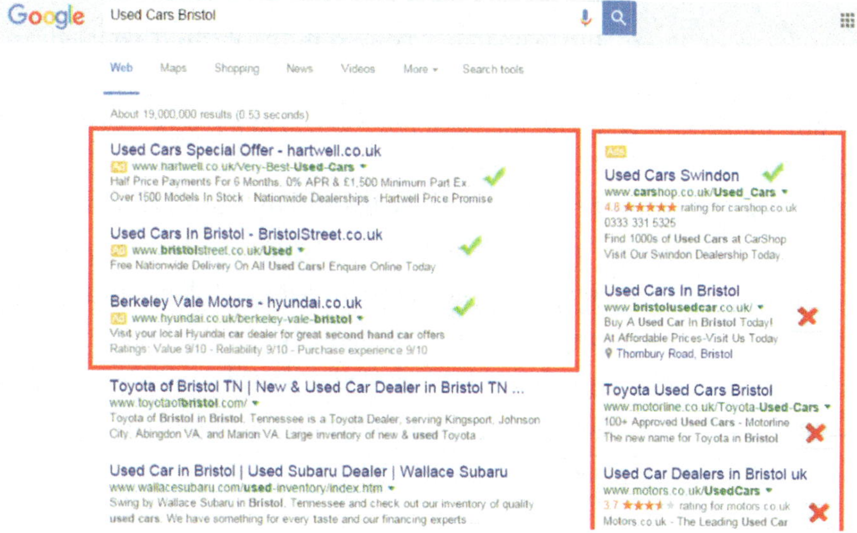

We have found that the further down the list they go, the higher the probability that you attract a price shopper that's literally clicking every single company along the way. You don't necessarily need to be the top listing, because that could just be a result of some random person that didn't think through what they're doing.

However, you want to maintain a top-four position. That's going to give you the best overall visibility, and ultimately, the best return on your investment. Pay attention to your average cost-per-click and manage your bids to maintain a top-four position.

Exact Match versus Broad Match

Pay attention to exact match versus broad match. There is a setting inside your AdWords campaign where you specify whether you want an exact match or a broad match.

Always Elect to do Exact Match

Why? If you choose "broad match," you could easily find yourself accidentally showing up on the search engines for many keywords that have nothing to do with your specific business.

Notice negative keywords – keywords that you don't want to show up for in the search engine. A great example of this is jobs, employment, marketing, etc. If someone types in "your city painter," that's great. If they type in "your city painting jobs," that's somebody looking for employment in the painting industry. Unless you are trying to fill a position or if you actually want to use your pay-per-click budget to get applicants, it's probably not the kind of person you want to attract.

What does it mean to set up negative keywords? As an example, if someone types in "jobs," "employment," or "marketing services" anywhere in their search, it pulls you out of that search and that specific bidding process, so you won't be paying for clicks from somebody that's not relevant to you.

I talked a little bit about making sure that you've set up mobile pay-per-click campaigns. I've mentioned the major transition of people searching on their mobile device versus people searching on their computer.

Phone Searches versus Computer Searches

More and more people are accessing the internet via smart devices: iPhones, Androids, and tablets. The searcher is typically in a different mind-frame when they are searching from a phone rather than from the computer.

When you're searching from a phone, you often just want to get the information right away, and/or want your problem solved as soon as possible. You can set up a campaign to have click-to-call built into your mobile campaign.

In the image above there was a search conducted from a mobile device, "Personal Injury Attorney." Do you see the "Call" button towards the bottom? That's what we call a mobile PPC campaign with the click-to-call function turned on.

When somebody hits that call button, they connect immediately with that law firm. It's a quick alternative to searching for the website and the phone number on your own, and as you can see, a mobile phone does not have much screen space.

Those pay-per-click listings become prominent and dominate the search results page on mobile. In many cases, you'll get the majority of the clicks if you're in those top two positions. It's all about convenience, and the click-to-call function allows that.

It's vital for your firm's success to connect with people who search from mobile devices. Set up a mobile-specific campaign and choose "Mobile Devices Only." Then, select your geolocation: your 30-mile range or 20-mile radius. Next, click a button to activate the click-to-call function.

That's how you establish a pay-per-click campaign that places you in the top positions if you bid correctly, with the option of a click-to-call.

To recap:

- Set up your ad groups correctly.
- Make sure to select keywords that group them together.
- Write text ads that speak directly to that group of keywords.

- Ensure your landing page (where you send those specific searches) speaks to the text ads and the group of keywords.

Feature a strong call-to-action that prompts your consumer into calling you as opposed to pressing the "Back" button and looking at four or five other competitors.

As the relevancy of your ad groups campaign and keywords improve, your cost-per-click will decline and conversions will increase. You can spend less and still achieve better positioning and more traffic to your website. When you follow these steps to maximize the profitability of your pay-per-click marketing campaigns, you will succeed in PPC where others fail.

GOOGLE LOCAL SERVICE ADS AND HOW THEY WORK

In late July of 2020, Google introduced Local Service Ads, "LSA's", to lawyers nationwide in the following practice areas: Bankruptcy, Business Law, Contract Law, Criminal Law, Disability Law, DUI, Estate Planning, Family Law, Immigration, Intellectual Property, Labor Law, Litigation, Malpractice, Personal Injury, Real Estate, Tax, and Traffic.

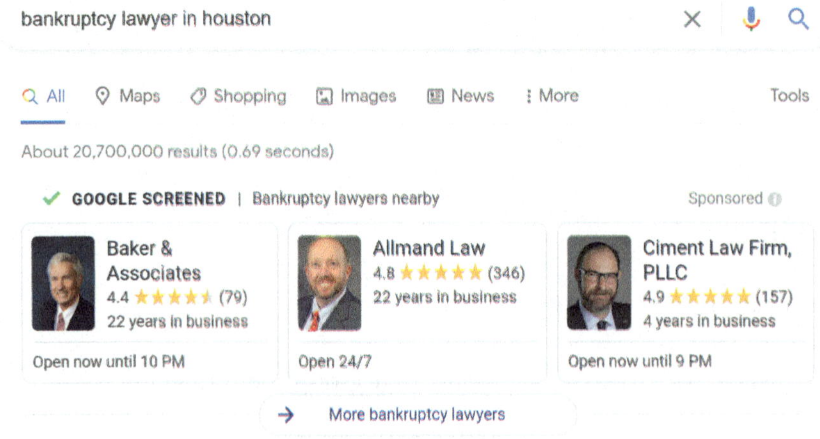

With Google Local Ads, you can make yourself visible to potential clients when they search for law firms like yours on Google Search and Maps. And you only pay for results, like clicks to your website or calls to your firm.

Here's how it works:

- ❖ You must complete the Google Local Services Application
- ❖ Google will run a background check on you and your employees
  - ➢ License check, background via Pinkerton Consulting, Insurance, etc.
  - ➢ Law firm owners must complete a background check
- ❖ Once approved and practicing in your geographical area, you will pay on a per-lead basis
  - ➢ We have seen between $25 and $45 per lead, but expect these prices to change over time
  - ➢ Price will vary by city and legal practice

As I mentioned, to get into Google Local Services, you must first complete an application. Google will conduct background checks on you and your employees through a company called Pinkerton. It can be an exhaustive process. In my experience, some law firms turn it around relatively quickly: they submit their documents, Google accepts them, and they are live. In other cases, depending on the firm's size, it can take up much more time.

HOW DOES GOOGLE CHARGE FOR SERVICES?

You set a weekly budget that limits the total amount of leads you receive in any given week. For example, $2,000 per month / $500 per week / $71 per day. Cost per lead equals $35. Fifty-seven leads per month / 14 leads per week / two per day. Once you spend the weekly budget, you go offline.

You may receive a different number of leads per day, but you never spend more than your designated weekly budget. If you receive an invalid lead, you can dispute it.

Once approved, your ads display on Google Local Service ads, and you pay on a per-lead basis. To sum it up, you set a weekly budget that you're willing to spend. Then Google carves it out based on the cost per lead.

In the example above, a $2,000 monthly budget divided by four results in a $500 weekly budget, equaling $71 per day. If the average cost per lead is $30 or $35, you won't appear in search results once you get one or two leads.

The good news? You only pay on a per-lead basis, with a relatively low cost per lead. The bad news? If you don't have a big enough budget, Google will quickly remove you from the results. Therefore, allocate as much money as possible to your budget if you have the capacity. Remember, your rotation in the top three results only remains active as long as your budget allows. You may receive a different amount of leads daily, but you will never spend more on any given week than the amount you have allocated to your budget.

As discussed, you can dispute a lead that is not valid. If a prospective client calls your office, but they are outside your designated service area or don't need a lawyer who practices in your law area, Google will not charge you for these leads. They have an excellent dispute process for these scenarios. In addition, should you receive a call from a solicitor, Google will work with you on these calls, from what we have seen.

FEEDBACK FROM ACTIVE USERS

- Lower cost per lead than PPC

- Still get some price shoppers and must follow up quickly
- Solid ROI from most of the clients that have chosen LSA

Based on our feedback from lawyers in various markets, it has a lower cost-per-lead than pay-per-click. On average, the lead quality is excellent because these prospective clients searched on Google for an attorney that practices in your area of law, not random lead sources across the Web.

Still, you will get price shoppers just as you do with Google ads and any other method of attracting qualified leads to your law firm. However, generally speaking, Google LSA provides a good ROI.

WHY IS THIS A NO-BRAINER FOR ATTORNEYS?

- Appear at the top of the results where your prospective clients are looking
- Only pay on a per-lead basis
- Lower cost-per-lead than PPC
- Ability to modify your budget based on schedule

Overall, Google LSA is a no-brainer for attorneys and law firms from coast to coast. Who wouldn't want to show up at the top where their prospective clients are searching? If they are searching on Google, we've got the local service ads, pay-per-click ads, organic ads, and other directories like Lawyers.com. If nothing else, being in Local Service Ads with the right strategy and budget allows you to show up at that point of the buying decision.

Since you only pay on a per-lead basis, you only pay for a qualified lead, and as I mentioned, the lead quality is excellent. Because it is flexible, Google LSA enables you to modify your budget based on your schedule. If your caseload is so high that all of your attorneys are too busy serving existing clients to take on new ones, you can reduce or pause your budget. Conversely, if things are slow at the firm and you want to attract more clients, you can increase the budget to keep the leads flowing. It's essential to manage the metrics and know your average conversion cost. To me, it's a no-brainer to go all-in and be as aggressive with Google LSA as you can.

How does the background verification work?

Another reason that LSAs are so different from PPC ads is because Google requires the Attorney to be verified. In order for your firm to get listed in one of these ads, Google needs to make sure that you are who you say you are, and are a barred attorney. Google checks your law license and bar number and verifies that you have the required insurance. Once Google has verified you, your LSA is connected to your Google Business Profile. To have it connected also requires that your firm have a minimum of one real client review, and your average star rating must be between 3 to 5 stars. Once all of these requirements are satisfied, you can build your dashboard and start to bid on leads.

SETTING UP GOOGLE LSA

If you're not on Google LSA already, there are two scenarios: if it's not in your area, get on the waitlist, or if it's active in your area, but you're not on it yet, submit your application to start the mandatory background check.

Does this sound confusing and time-consuming? Let us help you. We can't flip a switch, but we can gather the details, point you in the right direction, and partner with you through the process. Ultimately, make sure you sign up by clicking here: https://ads.google.com/local-services-ads/

CHAPTER THIRTEEN

Paid Online Directories — What Paid Online Directories Should You Consider Advertising in (Yelp, Foursquare, Yellow Pages, Better Business Bureau, Merchant Circle, etc.)

We talked about the overall internet marketing strategy, beginning with the foundation of a properly optimized website. We have also discussed how to set up the right pages on your website, conversion elements, off-page optimization for building inbound links, building authority for your domain, the review acquisition strategy, and ranking in the organic, non-pay-per-click listings for your most important keywords.

We then examined social media and email marketing as a vehicle to connect with your clients on a deeper level and obtain more repeated referral business. As you establish the non-paid elements of your internet marketing strategy, begin to consider paid online marketing programs. In the last chapter, we discussed pay-per-click marketing and how to implement an effective pay-per-click marketing campaign on AdWords or Microsoft Bing search to show up in the paid listings.

In this chapter, we'll cover **Paid Online Directory** listings. Paid online directory listings are among the most important to get premium listings. There are hundreds of online directories, from Justia and Martindale-Hubbell, to Lawyers.com and FindLaw.com.

Let's focus on the biggest, the ones that will help your law firm **gain exposure** where your prospective clients are browsing the web most often.

Paid Online Directory Listings and Online Sites You Should Consider

According to Rankings.io, the best lawyer directories include:

- FindLaw
- Avvo
- Super Lawyers
- Justia
- Nolo
- Martindale-Hubbell

If you have an unlimited budget and your organics are doing well, I recommend that you consider paying for premium placement in these online directories.

FindLaw.com

FindLaw.com is a free legal information website that helps consumers, small-business owners, students, and legal professionals find answers to everyday legal questions and legal counsel when necessary. The site includes case law, state and federal statutes, a lawyer directory, and legal news and analysis.

It also includes a free legal dictionary and magazine called Writ, whose contributors (mostly legal academics) argue, explain and debate legal matters of topical interest.

FindLaw offers website development and Internet advertising services for legal professionals and extended members of the legal community through lawyermarketing.com.

Avvo.com

Avvo.com is an online marketplace for legal services, that provides lawyer referrals and access to a database of legal information consisting primarily of previously answered questions. Lawyer profiles may include client reviews, disciplinary actions, peer endorsements, and lawyer-submitted legal guides.

Avvo was founded in Seattle, Washington in 2006 by Mark Britton, a former legal counsel for Expedia, Inc. Britton said he developed the idea while vacationing in Italy and was still receiving inquiries from friends and colleagues seeking legal advice. Rich Barton, the founder of the Expedia, Inc. and real-estate database Zillow.com, was a key advisor during the initial ideation stages and still serves on the board of directors. Avvo was derived from "avvocato", the Italian word for lawyer.[3]

Super Lawyers

Super Lawyers is a rating service of outstanding lawyers from more than 70 practice areas who have attained a high degree of peer recognition and professional achievement. The patented selection process is multi-phased and includes independent research, peer nominations, and peer evaluations.

Super Lawyers magazine features the list and profiles of selected attorneys and is distributed to attorneys in the state or region and the ABA-accredited law school libraries. Super Lawyers is also published as a special section in leading city and regional magazines across the country. Visit one of the web's most trusted online attorney directories at SuperLawyers.com.

Justia.com

Justia is an American website specializing in legal information retrieval. It was founded in 2003 by Tim Stanley, formerly of FindLaw, and is one of the largest online databases of legal cases. The company is headquartered in Mountain View, California.[1] The website offers free case law, codes, opinion summaries, and other basic legal texts, with paid services for its attorney directory and web hosting.[2][3]

In 2007, the New York Times reported that Justia was spending around "$10,000 a month" in order "to copy documents" from the United States Supreme Court and publish them online, to be made available without the public paying fees.[4] Law library research guides often refer to Justia. Duke Law School's law library's research guide notes how it's helpful for PACER.[5]

Nolo.com

Nolo, formerly known as Nolo Press, is a publisher in Berkeley, California, that produces do-it-yourself legal books and software that allows people to handle simple legal matters such as making wills or writing business partnership contracts.[4] Its areas of focus include immigration, family law, employment law, tenant and landlord issues, wills, trusts, and intellectual property.[5] Even though Nolo encourages consumers and small business owners to handle their own legal matters when it is reasonably feasible to do so, the company recommends getting professional legal help for disputable or difficult matters.

The company was founded in an attic in 1971 by Ralph Warner (a graduate of UC Berkeley's Boalt School of Law) and family law attorney Ed Sherman. The company's logo shows the scales of justice tilted in favor of the reader, and includes the motto "LAW for ALL."

Martindale-Hubbell

Martindale-Hubbell is an information services company to the legal profession that was founded in 1868. The company publishes the Martindale-Hubbell Law Directory, which provides background information on lawyers and law firms in the United States and other countries. It also published the Martindale Hubbell Law Digest, a summary of laws around the world. Martindale-Hubbell is owned by consumer website company Internet Brands.[1]

Pay-Per-Lead and Lead Services and the Legal Profession

Many lawyers wonder if it is ethical to buy leads, concerned that doing so would get them into trouble with the American Bar Association. According to Fuellead.com, per the American Bar Association Rule 7.2, lawyers can buy leads:

"[5] A lawyer may pay others for generating client leads, such as Internet-based client leads, as long as the lead generator does not recommend the lawyer, any payment to the lead generator is consistent with Rules 1.5(e) (division of fees) and 5.4 (professional independence of the lawyer), and the lead generator's communications are consistent with Rule 7.1 (communications concerning a lawyer's services). To comply with Rule 7.1, a lawyer must not pay a lead generator that states, implies, or creates a reasonable impression that it is recommending the lawyer, is making the referral without payment from the lawyer, or has analyzed a person's legal problems when determining which lawyer should receive the referral."

The article goes on to state:

"...as long as the lead generation company (the third-party company that's generating the lead – by lead I mean somebody who has visited a third-party company's website and filled out a form asking for a free consultation with an attorney to discuss a particular legal problem) doesn't specifically recommend or make claims about the legal expertise/qualifications of their law firm client, and discloses to the person asking for help that the lawyers receiving the leads have paid to participate and that no legal assessment of their situation has been made by filling out the form, buying leads is ethical for lawyers.

"A lead is just an inquiry and somebody who wants to discuss their situation with a legal professional. In this scenario, the lead generation company is merely the conduit through which the consumer, the person looking for an attorney, can find somebody to speak to about their legal issue.

"Also Rule 7.1 is referenced in the ABA rule 7.2 – 7.1 says you can pay for leads which, which States to comply with rule 7.1 a lawyer must not pay a lead generator that states, implies, or creates a reasonable impression that it's recommending the lawyer making the referral without payment, or that it is attempting to analyze the person's legal problems. Effectively what that means is that any of the generation companies can sell leads to a lawyer as long as a few things happen.

"First, the lead generation company cannot specifically recommend the lawyer. So, a landing page or a website for a lead generation company can say:

"'Get a free consultation with a local auto accident attorney to discuss your claim'.

"However, it cannot say:

"'Get a free consultation with Jones and Smith…The best personal injury attorneys in the state of California!'

"That would be against the American Bar Association's rules, as it's creating a reasonable impression that the lead generator is recommending the client. If it's generic, and it simply says you may be entitled to compensation – if you'd like a free consultation with an auto accident attorney, please fill out our form and we will have somebody to contact you. Makes a big difference in that you're not recommending any one specific firm."

How Do Pay-Per-Lead Services Work?

The benefit of using a pay-per-lead service is that you only pay when you get a qualified lead. With others, you have a budget; for example, you set aside $500.00/month to get all of the leads that come in from that area. Most of these pay-per-lead service providers have combined experience in a wide range of industries including law, healthcare, and home improvement.

If you have followed the plan outlined in this book, your organic keywords ought to be ranking well in the search engines and map listings. You should have established proactive social media and email marketing strategies and a well-structured pay-per-click marketing campaign. If you want to bump the lead flow, these services can help to start channeling new people that are in the market for your firm's practice areas.

However, you must be diligent and quick to respond.

You will hear many horror stories about how badly these lead services work and the amount of money you can waste on them. Let me be the first to advise, this is not the place to start. If you have built your internet marketing strategy on pay-per-lead services, you're destined to fail. You can't build a sustainable business around this one strategy alone.

But, as an add-on to a strong internet marketing program, the service can be somewhat effective. The key is to remember that these requests for leads aren't coming to you directly. They're on Emfluence and Fuel Lead.

The potential client sends an anonymous request for a quote and provides their name and email address, knowing they will receive phone calls. However, they are most likely price-conscious shoppers who use this service because they want the lowest price possible. Keep that in mind.

Fast Follow Up Is Critical

These leads also go out to you and a number of other firms in your area, which means you must be aggressive. You must be the first person to get the potential clients on the phone, be professional, and make a compelling offer that inspires them to choose you over your competition.

You must also **create a follow-up system** to ensure you have a fallback plan in place for leads you can't reach right away. You can get these leads in a variety of formats. They'll send you an email, you can login and download an Excel list, or you can receive a text message alert as soon as the email comes through.

If you have a marketing manager on your team, be sure to assign a specific person to follow up on leads.

Know who is accountable for these leads when they come in.

If it's going to you, to your dispatcher, or even one of your paralegals or other administrators, avoid any confusion about who is responsible for following up because then the lead falls through the cracks.

Assign a specific person the responsibility of contacting these people and provide a predefined script describing how to handle the call. Be professional. Be courteous. Be quick.

A lot of these are going to go to the first person that gets them on the phone, so it is important to be aggressive. Don't just call once. Implement a process in which you reach out to these people three to five times over the course of the next 24 hours because they're in the window to buy.

Then, have a fallback strategy, in the event that you don't get them on the phone. In that case, take note of their name and email address so that you can remain top-of-mind with them. The reality is this is somebody in your service area that is in need of your specialty.

If you're not sending an email follow-up or adding them to your email marketing database, you're wasting marketing dollars. If you've just spent $5, $10, $25 for that lead and you're not proactively and diligently following up with them via email, you might as well not even pay for this service.

We have provided a script for you to develop a fallback strategy

Set up an email auto-responder on a program such as AWeber or Mailchimp, where your marketing manager can enter the client's name and email address and send out a series of emails to the client over the next several days.

Caution: do not let email become a crutch because they alone are not going to do the trick.

Email 1 – Subject – Your Recent XYZ Service Inquiry

Client Name,
You recently submitted a request on [LEAD Site] for help with XYZ Law Firm. I called and left a message for you on the number that was listed and look forward to talking with you soon. You can reach me directly at xxx-xxx-

xxxx. With so many personal injury law firms to choose from in [YOUR CITY], I know it can be hard to know who you can trust.

At XYZ Law Firm we have been serving the [your city] area since 1982 and are dedicated to resolving your XYZ issue quickly and cost-effectively. Give me a call at xxx-xxx-xxxx to schedule your consultation.

Email 2 – Special Offer for XYZ Services

Client Name,

You indicated that you were in need of some XYZ legal services a few days ago. I'm sure you have received a number of calls from XYZ Law Firm, who are eager to earn your business.

Email 3 – Subject – RE: Your Recent Business Inquiry

Client Name,

You reached out to us earlier this week via [lead site] looking for some help. We would love to be of service to you. I have tried you a few times on the phone number you listed with no success and don't know if you are just busy or if you already hired another law firm. Please send me a quick reply to let me know if we can be of assistance or give me a call at xxx-xxx-xxxx.

The aggressive follow-up work on the phone will get you the business. Use email as a fallback strategy.

Stay in Touch

Again, don't stop there. You've acquired the client's name and email address with consent to email them. Continue marketing to these clients via email on at least a monthly basis. Maintain an email database of clients and prospects you send emails to once a month with some type of update.

"Here's what's going on with our firm. Here's why you should consider our firm's services". Creating a connection even after the case is closed is critical to giving clients a sense of ease and letting them know your firm has them in mind.

This strategy is critical if you want your firm to remain top-of-mind so that you can build your client base both in email and social media.

As you look at paid online advertising and paid-per-lead services, be cautious. Don't overspend. Put the tracking in place to make sure you've got a strong return on investment. If you are going to implement the pay-per-lead service strategy, implement a proactive, diligent process that touches these people multiple times, via phone and email.

CHAPTER FOURTEEN

Track, Measure AND Quantify – How to Track Your Online Marketing Plan to Ensure That Your Investment is Generating a Strong Return on Investment

Congratulations! Now That You Have…

- Built and optimized your website;
- Put an ongoing link building strategy in place where you're creating inbound links and moving up in the search engines;

- Implemented email marketing and social media marketing initiatives; and

Possibly implemented a paid online marketing campaign including Pay-Per-Click and Pay-Per-Lead services...

...You must put tools in place to track, measure, and quantify your data to ensure you're moving in a positive direction.

- Google Analytics
  www.google.com/analytics
- Keyword Tracking Report
  www.gshiftlabs.com
- Call Tracking Report -
  www.callfire.com

Analytics Tracking

There are multiple tracking mechanisms you can put in place. I recommend these three core tracking mechanisms:

- Google Analytics
- Keyword Tracking

Call Tracking

Google Analytics is an excellent website data analysis tool and it's completely free. It will reveal:

- How many visitors got to your website on a daily, weekly, monthly, and annual basis

- What keywords they typed in to get there

- What pages on your website they visited
- How long they stayed

The most critical piece of information you want from Google Analytics is where you started and where you are now.

Ask yourself, "When I started this whole internet marketing process, how many visitors was I getting to my website?" Maybe it was five, 20, 100, or 500, but it's good to know. Then you can compare to future data on an ongoing basis.

Ultimately, you want to determine if the amount of visitors to your website is increasing. Is the variety of keywords consumers use to find you increasing? Are you moving in a positive direction?

You can also set up reports within Google Analytics. To open an account on Google Analytics, visit Google.com/analytics. It's a simple process in which you verify you own the website through a variety of different methods, then install a small piece of code into your website's HTML. After you have done that, the tracking is in place and you are ready to go.

SAMPLE GOOGLE ANALYTICS TRAFFIC REPORT

Traffic Overview:

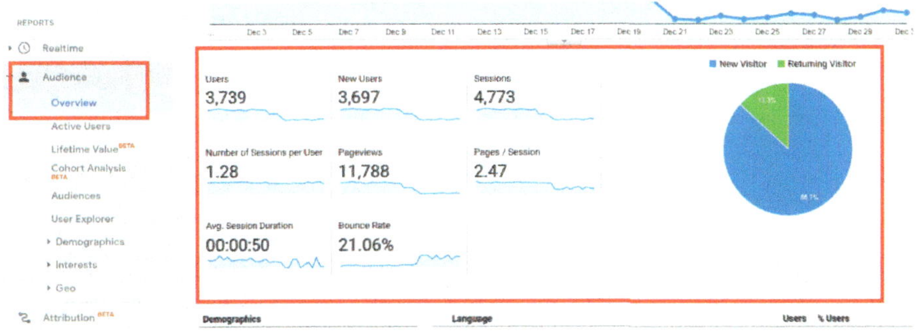

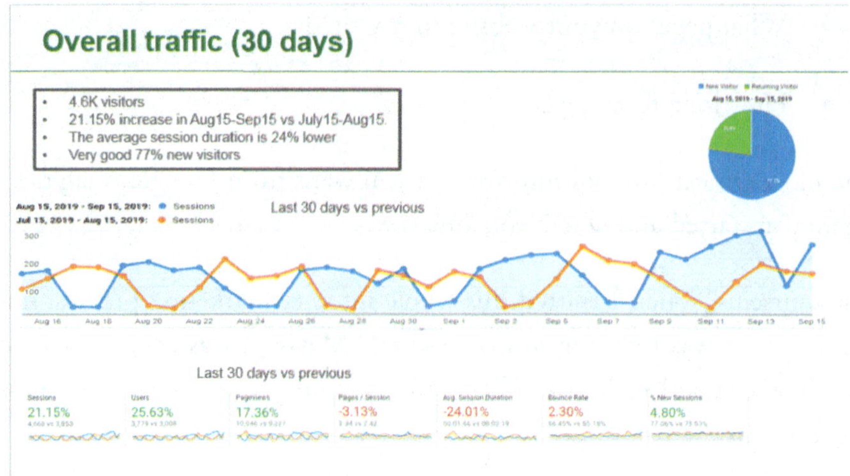

Traffic by Page:

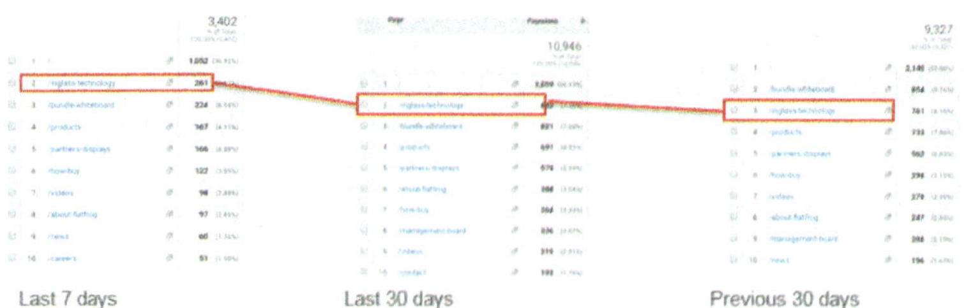

Traffic by Location:

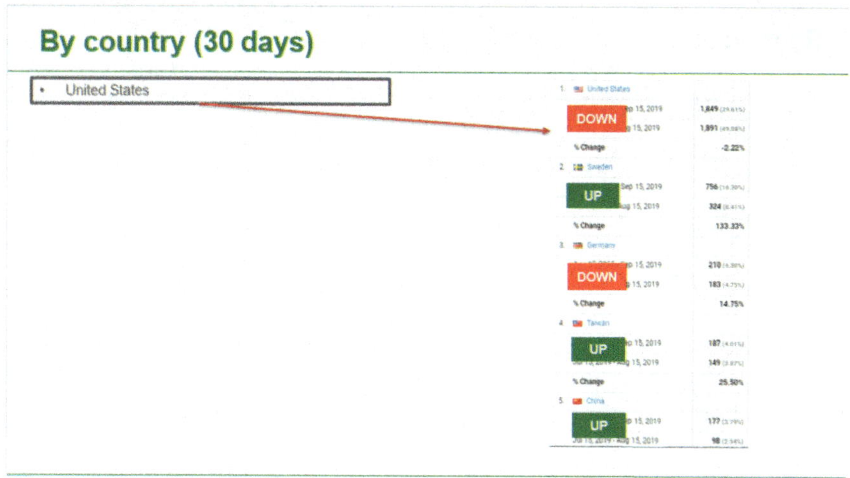

Traffic Flow:

Traffic by Device:

By device

- 81% of the media is desktop
- 59% of desktop is Chrome
- 59% of mobile is iOS

Demographics:

Demographic (30 days)

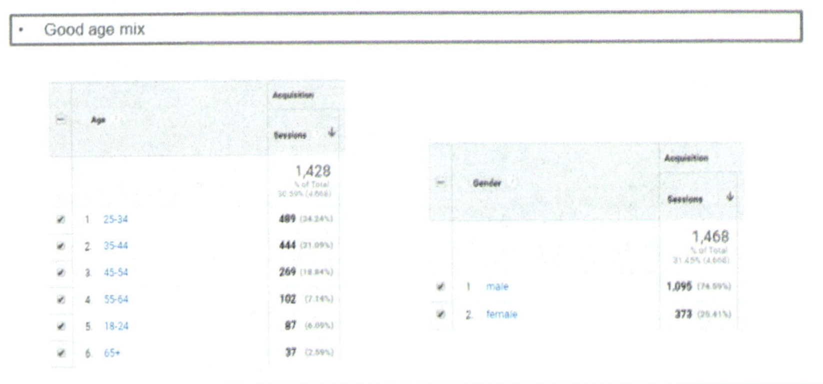

	Age	Acquisition: Sessions
		1,428 % of Total
1	25-34	489
2	35-44	444
3	45-54	269
4	55-64	102
5	18-24	87
6	65+	37

	Gender	Acquisition: Sessions
		1,468 % of Total
1	male	1,095
2	female	373

Keyword Tracking

The other tracking mechanism I recommend is keyword tracking.

At the beginning of this process, we talked about keyword research to determine what keywords people type when they need your legal services.

We came up with a list and all those keywords were combined with your cities and sub-cities.

There are tools that will tell you how you're ranking on Google, Yahoo, and Bing for those various keywords. A few options include:

- Bright Local
- White Spark
- Raven Tools
- WebCEO

BrightLocal

I recommend BrightLocal as a keyword tracking tool.

You can learn more about it at www.brightlocal.com. There is a cost associated with this service, but it is a wonderful resource for tracking your search engine optimization progress.

Put your keywords into the BrightLocal Keyword Tracker, then set up a weekly and monthly report that shows where you rank on Google, Yahoo, and Bing for your most important keywords.

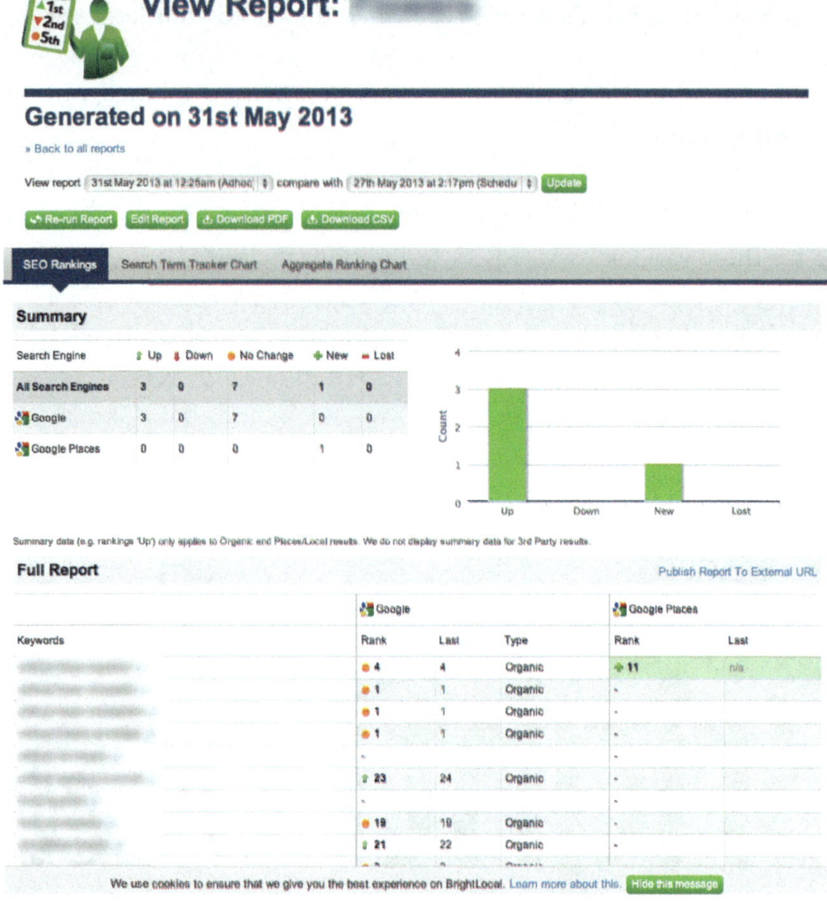

With a report like this, you can easily see how your website is trending in the search engines.

You'll see yourself move up in the results if you've built the website correctly with the right on-page factors (title tags, H1 tags, meta descriptions, etc.); if you're building links; developing citations; and have a proactive review acquisition system in place.

If you are stagnating, you can go back to that keyword, figure out which page is optimized for it, look at your links and link profile, and whatever is necessary to push that keyword to the next level.

Call Tracking

The third vital tracking mechanism I recommend is call tracking. Achieving better rankings and more visits to your website is an excellent start, but in most businesses, nothing happens until a qualified prospect makes a call.

Calls are crucial to your business. Therefore, put some type of tracking mechanism in place to determine how many calls are coming in on a monthly basis and what's happening within those conversations.

Are calls turning into sales? That's where the rubber meets the road. That's why we're doing all of this. Who cares if you're in the number one position if it doesn't result in dollars to the firm?

Here are a few of several call tracking tools you can use:

- CallFire
- DialogTech
- CallSource
- Century Interactive

CallFire is one of the most popular. Learn more about it at CallFire.com.

Most of these call tracking services will let you choose a phone number based on your area code. So, you type in the number you want to get. It's a nominal fee on a monthly basis ($2-$5 per month), and you get a tracking number.

Then, you can put the tracking phone number on the graphics on your website to track the number of calls and even listen to recordings of the conversation.

That number will be set to ring in your office, just like a forwarding number. If somebody dials it, it still rings your office like always, but it is a tracking number.

You can report on the number of calls using the internet and playback recordings of those conversations. It's extremely powerful to know the number of calls you were getting when you started versus the number after you incorporated your new marketing strategy.

You can listen to those conversations and ascertain how many of those calls turned into a booked consultation while knowing the revenue associated with that service. That is how you obtain a true gauge of the return on investment associated with your online marketing strategy.

These are the types of tracking mechanisms I recommend. Analytics, keyword tracking, and call tracking give you the most important key performance indicators to monitor your progress.

CHAPTER FIFTEEN

Next Steps

WHAT'S NEXT?

Throughout the course of this book, we have covered an abundance of information.

We've mapped out your internet marketing plan and taken you step-by-step through how to claim and optimize your Google map listing, optimize your website for the most commonly searched keywords in your area and leverage social media to get more repeat and referral business.

We then covered paid online marketing strategies like pay-per-click and pay-per-lead services. If you have taken action and followed our instructions, you should be well on your way to dominating the search engines for the keywords in your area.

Need More Help?

If you've gotten to this point and feel like you need some extra help to implement these ideas, we are here to support you. As experts in helping law firms across the nation, we have had tremendous success implementing these strategies.

You can call us directly at 561-903-2832 with any questions you might have. Our team will review your entire online marketing effort (Website, Competition, Search Engine Placement, Social Media, etc.) and come back to you with a complete assessment of how you can improve and what you can do to take your online marketing efforts to the next level.

Request A Free Custom Online Marketing Evaluation Now

Your Custom-Tailored Optimization Audit will:

- Identify key issues that could be harming your website without you even knowing it.
- Look at where your website stands compared to your competitors.
- Determine whether SEO is the appropriate route for you to take.
- Uncover hidden revenue that you're leaving on the table.
- Offer recommendations that you can put to use immediately

Schedule your custom audit at www.lawfirmmarketingpros.com. Visit our Free Resources Page to download your Online Marketing Checklist for Law Firms.

Acknowledgments

There are so many people I can and should acknowledge who have helped me get to this stage of my life where I can share such a wealth of information with lawyers and their support staff — my readers. More recently, a few stand out who have helped make it happen. To Andy Leonard and Vince Gelormine, without you, I would not be here today. As I've stated so many times in the past, my daughter, Keri Danielle, I couldn't have done it without you. My sister Lisa Konigsberg-Elko thanks for your patience, motivation, and insight. Daria Anne DiGiovanni, you are the consummate professional; your experience and wisdom helped guide me through the difficult spots to complete the manuscript. The team at Law Firm Marketing Pros, whose editorial contributions kept me up-to-date with the ever-changing digital marketing ecosystem. Josh Nelson, no words can describe your impact on me, my family, and our industry; you are an inspiration to us all.

References

CHAPTER ONE

Martindale-Hubbell
https://www.martindale.com/

Lawyers.com
https://www.lawyers.com/

FindLaw.com
https://www.findlaw.com/

Avvo.com
https://www.avvo.com/

Super Lawyers
https://www.superlawyers.com/

2021 comparison of Google organic clickthrough rates (SEO CTR) by ranking position
https://www.smartinsights.com/search-engine-optimisation-seo/seo-analytics/comparison-of-google-clickthrough-rates-by-position/

47 Facebook Stats That Matter to Marketers in 2021:
https://blog.hootsuite.com/facebook-statistics/

71 Up-To-Date YouTube Statistics for Your Marketing Strategy In 2021
https://www.semrush.com/blog/youtube-stats/

CHAPTER THREE

Website by Tonight
https://websitebytonight.com/

GoDaddy
https://www.godaddy.com/

Ionos by 1 & 1
https://www.ionos.com/

WordPress
https://wordpress.com/

Joomla
https://launch.joomla.org/

Drupal
https://www.drupal.com/

CHAPTER FOUR

Googlebot
https://developers.google.com/search/docs/advanced/crawling/googlebot

Finding Information by Crawling
https://www.google.com/search/howsearchworks/crawling-indexing/#:~:text=Finding%20information%20by%20crawling&text=We%20use%20software%20known%20as,webpages%20back%20to%20Google%27s%20servers

Learn About Sitemaps
https://developers.google.com/search/docs/advanced/sitemaps/overview?hl=en&visit_id=637565243311186543-4189916316&rd=1

About Search Console
https://support.google.com/webmasters/answer/9128668?hl=en

Ask Google to Recrawl Your URLs
https://developers.google.com/search/docs/advanced/crawling/ask-google-to-recrawl?hl=en&visit_id=637565243610496141-1438526853&rd=1

Robots meta tag, data-nosnippet, and X-Robots-Tag specifications
https://developers.google.com/search/docs/advanced/robots/robots_meta_tag?hl=en

CHAPTER FIVE

Keyword Finder
https://app.kwfinder.com/

CHAPTER SIX

Google Business Profile
https://www.google.com/business/

List of the Top Citation Sources for Law Firms

Lawyers.com
http://www.lawyers.com/

Martindale
http://www.martindale.com/

Find Law
http://www.findlaw.com/

USLegal Lawyers
http://lawyers.uslegal.com/

Legal Webfinder
http://www.legalwebfinder.com/

List Lawyers
http://www.list-lawyers.com/

USA Attorneys
http://usattorneys.com/

HG
https://www.hg.org/

Attorney Directory Database
https://attorneydirectorydb.org/

Injury Lawyers
http://injurylawyers.jouwweb.nl/

Google Maps Help (Writing Reviews)
https://support.google.com/maps/answer/6230175?co=GENIE.Platform%3DDesktop&hl=en

Yelp.com, Write A Review
https://www.yelp.com/writeareview

Top-Rated Law Firm, Law Firm Marketing Pros
https://www.lawfirmmarketingpros.com/law-firm-reputation-monitoring-marketing/

Networking and Referral Expert Bob Burg
https://burg.com/

Marketing Myopia (Harvard Business Review Classics), Kindle Edition, Theodore Levitt
https://www.amazon.com/dp/B00UJZPFH4/ref=dp-kindle-redirect?_encoding=UTF8&btkr=1

CHAPTER SEVEN

What Is a Good Conversion Rate? The Answer Might Surprise You
https://www.crazyegg.com/blog/what-is-good-conversion-rate/

CHAPTER EIGHT

Up to 70% of web traffic happens on a mobile device, Tech Jury
https://techjury.net/blog/what-percentage-of-internet-traffic-is-mobile/#gref

80% of users used a mobile device to search the internet in 2019, Statista.com
https://www.statista.com/topics/779/mobile-internet/#dossierSummary

By 2020, the number of smartphone users is projected to reach 2.87 billion.
https://review42.com/resources/smartphone-statistics/#:~:text=100%20million%20people%20have%20started,smartphone%20users%20worldwide%20in%202020.

Almost three-quarters of internet users will be mobile-only by 2025
https://www.warc.com/content/paywall/article/warc-datapoints/almost_three_quarters_of_internet_users_will_be_mobileonly_by_2025/124845

The Ultimate Mobile Email Statistics Overview, Email Monday
https://www.emailmonday.com/mobile-email-usage-statistics/

101 Mobile Marketing Statistics and Trends For 2020 (Updated in January, 2021)
https://quoracreative.com/article/mobile-marketing-statistics

Mobile advertising spending worldwide from 2007 to 2022
https://www.statista.com/statistics/303817/mobile-internet-advertising-revenue-worldwide/

27 Eye-Opening Website Statistics: Is Your Website Costing You Clients?
https://www.sweor.com/firstimpressions

Your M-Commerce Deep Dive: Data, Trends and What's Next in the Mobile Retail Revenue World
https://www.bigcommerce.com/blog/mobile-commerce/#why-does-mobile-commerce-matter

50 Consumers Online Shopping Behavior Trends
https://brizfeel.com/consumer-online-retail-shopping-behavior/

Think with Google, Marketing Strategies, App and Mobile
https://www.thinkwithgoogle.com/marketing-strategies/app-and-mobile/b2b-search-statistics/

Device usage of Facebook users worldwide as of January 2021
https://www.statista.com/statistics/377808/distribution-of-facebook-users-by-device/

Google Mobile-Friendly Test
https://search.google.com/test/mobile-friendly

Your Firm App
https://yourfirmapp.com/

CHAPTER NINE

20 Facebook stats to guide your 2021 Facebook strategy
https://sproutsocial.com/insights/facebook-stats-for-marketers/

44 Instagram Stats That Matter to Marketers in 2021
https://blog.hootsuite.com/instagram-statistics/

Greathouse Trial Law Facebook Page
https://www.facebook.com/greathousetriallaw

Greathouse Trial Law Twitter Page
https://twitter.com/AtlTrialLaw

CHAPTER TEN

Law Firm Marketing Pros
https://www.lawfirmmarketingpros.com/

Personal Injury FAQs - Greathouse Trial Law
https://www.atltriallaw.com/personal-injury/personal-injury-faqs/

How Effective Are Email Newsletters for Marketing a Business? Campaign Monitor
https://www.campaignmonitor.com/resources/knowledge-base/how-effective-are-email-newsletters-for-marketing-a-business/

Clio
https://www.clio.com/

Lawyerist
https://lawyerist.com/

CASEpeer
https://www.casepeer.com/

Litify
https://www.litify.com/

Vimeo
https://vimeo.com/

Daily Motion
https://www.dailymotion.com/us

CHAPTER THIRTEEN

Legal Directories: Best Lawyer Directories (2020 List)
https://rankings.io/legal-directories/

FindLaw.com
https://www.findlaw.com/

Avvo.com
https://www.avvo.com/

SuperLawyers.com
https://www.superlawyers.com/

Justia.com
https://www.justia.com/

Nolo.com
https://www.nolo.com/

Martindale Hubbell
https://www.martindale.com/

FuelLead.com
https://www.fuellead.com/can-lawyers-buy-leads/#:~:text=In%20a%20short%20answer%20yes,others%20to%20recommend%20a%20lawyer

Rule 7.2: Communications Concerning a Lawyer's Services: Specific Rules - Comment, American Bar Association
https://www.americanbar.org/groups/professional_responsibility/publications/model_rules_of_professional_conduct/rule_7_2_advertising/comment_on_rule_7_2/

Emfluence
https://emfluence.com/#gref

BrightLocal
https://www.brightlocal.com/

CallFire
https://www.callfire.com/

Law Firm Marketing Pros Free Resources Page
https://www.lawfirmmarketingpros.com/free-tools/

Pay-Per-Click
https://en.wikipedia.org/wiki/Pay-per-click

Web Crawler
https://en.wikipedia.org/wiki/Web_crawler

Made in the USA
Coppell, TX
13 February 2026

71314143R00134